PIER LUIGI NERVI

THE MASTERS OF
WORLD ARCHITECTURE SERIES
UNDER THE GENERAL EDITORSHIP OF WILLIAM ALEX

pier luigi nervi

by *Ada Louise Huxtable*

DISTRIBUTED BY POCKET BOOKS, INC.

George Braziller, Inc.

NEW YORK, 1960

CONTENTS

ACKNOWLEDGEMENTS

Appreciation is expressed to Pier Luigi Nervi, whose interest and cooperation have made this book possible; to Burton H. Holmes, who kindly read the manuscript in his capacity as a technical expert; to *Progressive Architecture,* of the Reinhold Publishing Company, for permission to reprint sections of a Nervi review by the author; to the F. W. Dodge Corporation, for the use of quotations from "Structures," by P. L. Nervi, © 1956 by F. W. Dodge Corporation, translation of Nervi's book, "Costruire Correttamentee"; to Charles Magruder for constant encouragement; and to my understanding and helpful family.

INTRODUCTION

When PIER LUIGI NERVI speaks of his work, it is with matter-of-fact modesty. To questions about the technical innovations of the unprecedented structures that he has built for almost half a century, he replies, in a tone of slight surprise: "It was simple . . . the obvious solution . . . the logical thing to do."

From even the most superficial examination of his work, however, it is evident that Nervi's solutions go far beyond the obvious: his uniquely personal, intricate structural logic has established a creative highpoint in 20th century engineering and architectural design. Unlike many gifted people, he feels no need to press proof of his genius upon the public, for his work speaks eloquently for him. The clarity of its structure and the grace of its forms combine to give new meaning to the unfashionable word "beauty."

Nervi's stature in the field of engineering design is acknowledged internationally. Now that the postwar hoopla about the "rebirth" of Italian creativity has died down, we see much of the widely publicized "renaissance" as a self-conscious, slightly hysterical straining after originality for its own sake. (One thing that the Italians have never lost, and that needed no postwar revival, is a dramatic flair for striking theatrical poses.) Today, the quality of Nervi's work stands alone, in the truly great tradition of Italian design.

Nor is it odd that this tradition, based largely on an elegant array of magnificent palaces and churches, should turn to factories, hangars, warehouses and exposition halls. It is in these buildings that we find the current frontiers of design, and the most significant structural and esthetic advances of our age. Their unprecedented and unconventional requirements offer the most challenging opportunities to explore the basic problem of the enclosure of space. Nervi's most successful designs, all space constructions of primary significance, are outstanding contributions to the solution of this problem—the Florence Stadium, 1930–32; the series of airplane hangers at Orvieto, Orbetello and Torre del Lago, 1936–41; the Turin Exposition Hall, 1948–49; a salt warehouse at Tortona, 1950–51; a tobacco factory at Bologna, 1952; a wool factory in Rome, 1953; the Fiat Works in Turin, 1955; and the 1960 Olympic buildings in Rome.

Perhaps the key to Nervi's stature as a designer lies in the fact that although his structure is intricate, and often decorative, it is never arbitrary or obscure. His buildings are most remarkable for the clarity of their engineering. The power and grace of these extraordinary shapes and patterns stem directly from their structural logic, and are inseparable from it. It is possible even for the layman to feel tension and compression, the direction of forces, and the inevitable, correct relationship of structure to shape. The elegant contours of the cantilevered roof trusses of the Florence Stadium, (plate 6) for example, are clearly dictated by the concentration of load and reinforcement; and the great arched ribs of the Turin Exposition Hall (plate 26) gather their forces visibly in the fan-shaped ribs at the sides of the hall and transfer these forces to the ruggedly handsome buttresses below. This kind of dynamic structural beauty is one of architecture's greatest sensory satisfactions. The fusion of structural function and abstract form creates a kind of building that is so fundamentally right that most other architecture seems superficial beside it.

With a clear design logic, Nervi believes in "the inherent esthetic force of a good structural solution." It would be well for architects to consider his warning that "a good structural organism worked out passionately in detail and in general appearance is essential to good architecture."[1] They might note the word "passionately," too, for although only a Latin would dare to use it, it implies a state of heart and mind necessary to all great works of art.

I

THE NATURE OF architecture has been discussed for centuries. Whether it is art or structure, esthetics or engineering—or, if a combination of both, in what proportion—is a constant challenge and a continuing subject of debate.

This was not always so. Although the questions themselves are timeless, the confusion about them is actually of comparatively recent origin. In Rome, the role of the architect uncompromisingly encompassed all of the activities of the engineer. Vitruvius, in his work *On Architecture,* written between 25 and 23 B.C., noted that the architect's responsibilities included building, mechanics, and—not the least of the mechanical arts of his time—clock making, with a special admonition that building must take equal account of strength (structure), utility (function), and grace (art). The office records of Villard de Honnecourt, in the year 1235, make it clear that the "master builder" of medieval times was still both architect and engineer, and from Leon Battista Alberti's definitive architectural treatise of 1451–52, we learn that the Renaissance brought no division of labor. The many-sided Renaissance man, in fact, considered all art his province, and all engineering a part of art—as witness the remarkable Leonardo, whose particular genius only magnified the accepted attitudes of his time.

"Him I call an architect," wrote Alberti, going far beyond mere matters of building, "who, by sure and wonderful Art and Method, is able both with Thought and Invention to devise and with Execution to compleat all those Works which, by means of the Movement of great Weights, and the Conjunction and Amassment of Bodies, can with the greatest beauty be adapted to the Uses of Mankind. And to be able to do this, he must have a thorough Insight into the Noblest and most curious Sciences . . ."[2] For not only were science and beauty still considered natural companions, but Renaissance thought predated some of the best-publicized "organic" architectural theory of the 20th century—as propounded by Frank Lloyd Wright—and pre-visualized some of the most remarkable effects of the structures made possible by the contemporary development of reinforced concrete—as a glance at the work of Pier Luigi Nervi in this book will testify.

That the Baroque architect worked in the same tradition is evidenced by such feats as Domenico Fontana's raising of the 75 foot, 327 ton obelisk in front of St. Peter's, for Pope Sixtus V, an undertaking that undoubtedly seemed as logical to him as the detailing of the facade of the Royal Palace at Naples. Not until the Age of Reason, with its philosophical and practical emphasis on "pure" science, and on the importance of experimental research for the development of scientific law, does the first sign of the split between architecture and engineering appear. As empirical rationalism and the veneration of isolated facts took over the age, natural and applied science moved into the field of technology and industry, and out of the realm of art. The 18th century laid the groundwork for the professional engineer. Coulomb, for example, undertook the mathematical investigation of structural statics in 1776, calculating with an accuracy impossible at an earlier date the earth pressure against revetment walls and the number and direction of forces and the points of fracture in certain vaults. The 19th century, in turn, saw highly accelerated progress in structural science. Integral calculus and solid geometry were developed as technical aids in the field of mathematics; scientific technology was introduced to construction to create the unprecedented field of engineering architecture. Polytechnic schools sprang up in France, Germany and Austria, training technicians in the use of the new scientific calculations, soon applied to revolutionary building materials: iron, steel and concrete. In America, particularly, no dream was too big, no ideal too ambitious for practical realization. The field of experimental, progressive construction, of untried techniques and unfamiliar forms, belonged exclusively to the engineer—the builder of bridges, factories, railroad sheds and exposition halls. The schism was complete. The architect, disturbed by, or oblivious to, the unorthodox methods and effects of his "scientific" colleagues, withdrew in self-righteous superiority to the peculiar refuge of the time: the ivory tower of the arts.

For the 19th century not only set Art and Science against each other; it was a period of singular paradox. An era of color, vigor and power, it preferred the pallid and the picturesque. It praised progress while it increasingly revered the past. Its real achievements were ignored for an effete, artificial, backward-looking culture; scientific and technological advances were carefully disguised with an overlay of approved "arty" pretentions. While the magnificent Corliss engines stood naked and gleaming at the Philadelphia Centennial Exposition of 1876, other remarkable products made possible by the vast new range of machinery—pretentiously labeled "the arts of manufacture" —were camouflaged in elaborate imitation of hand-made predecessors. Ornate nymphs and muses embraced tables, chairs, teapots and whatnots with the avowed purpose of esthetic and moral elevation. Behind the genteel Victorian "front," however, mores were realistic and ruthless. The new business leaders won wealth and power with a notorious lack of *politesse,* and courted respectability by overt and often ostentatious patronage of the arts. Seeking cultural status and security in the midst of social, economic and industrial upheaval, patron, public and architect endorsed an architecture that was a series of variations on respected traditional styles. They accepted formulas that eventually became frozen by academic rule for an impressive (if largely anti-structural) body of building of monumental clichés. Buildings were judged by the number, variety and originality of superficially applied orders; the structural elements beneath the external details were the age's "unmentionables." Architecture, once the master of all the building, mechanical and structural arts, was reduced to a correct veneer. Engineering was excluded from the respectable realm of art.

The technological revolution in progress, however, was to upset the whole tidy rule-book of Victorian architectural definition. Nor were the best minds of the 19th century unaware of the meaning of the new materials and techniques. "Architecture and construction must be taught, or practiced, simultaneously," said Viollet-le-Duc, one of the towering architectural arbiters of the age; "construction is the means, architecture is the result." [3] This succinct summation of the timeless essence of architecture was a rare statement in its day, suggesting the way to a renewed understanding of the art of building, in which technology and esthetics played an equal part. If he had this vision, however, it was still premature; most of his esteemed contemporaries did not share it. Ruskin defined architecture as the "decoration" of the facade, and his point of view was universally sustained. Even Viollet-le-Duc, architect, scholar, philosopher and gentleman in the best aristocratic-cultural tradition of his day, was not proof against the peculiar, polite dualism that characterized the Victorian outlook: he was at once an ardent pioneer of the beginnings of modern metal construction and a dedicated champion of correct medieval revivalism. Nor was he aware of any ambiguity in his attitudes, or in those of his times.

While the best architects toyed with Gothic and Romanesque revivals and the "French taste" swept Europe and America, the engineers built the monuments of the 19th century. In England, Thomas Telford's early iron bridges (the proposal for the Thames Bridge, with Douglas, was made in 1801) opened a totally new field of construction: the use of cast- and wrought-iron for structures and spans of unprecedented size and strength. Watt and Boulton's utilization of cast-iron beams and columns, for a mill at Manchester, also in 1801, and bridge-engineer William Fairbairn's improvements incorporating wrought-iron plates and beams in the '40's prepared the way for the modern industrial plant. Huge, iron-arched railway sheds appeared commonly from the 1850's to the 1890's; London's St. Pancras Station, built in 1866, set a record span of 210 feet. By mid-century, engineering moved openly into the field of architecture in the great exposition buildings, beginning with one of the most significant structures of the Victorian Age—William Paxton's celebrated Crystal Palace of 1851. This famous glass and iron building, designed and executed by a gardener-engineer, presaged the prefabrication and demountability of metal frame construction that has totally revolutionized the structure and the design of the architecture of the 20th century. The engineers' exposition architecture, in fact, sustained building progress for the next 50 years, from the 157 foot span of the Palais de l'Industrie of the 1855 Paris Exposition to the 375 foot span of Cottancin and Dutert's Galerie des Machines in the Paris Fair of 1889, culminating in Eiffel's timeless tower for the same exhibition. In America, bridge construction, based on English, French and German developments, leapt forward with singular daring: James B. Eads' St. Louis Bridge, 1868–74, built almost entirely of steel, initiated requirements for a material for which no standards yet existed; John and Washington Roebling's Brooklyn Bridge, 1600 feet in length and the world's longest suspension span in 1883, was, and still is, an engineering triumph and a work of art. The experiments and calculations of the bridge engineers led logically to the evolution of the contemporary steel-framed skyscraper—a unique American development centered in Chicago in the '80's. Steel beams introduced into the iron frame of the Home Insurance Building of 1883–84 made the unlimited multistoried building a reality, and changed the skyline of the world.

Occasionally, an architect appeared who understood the significance of the new engineering, and used it well. Louis Sullivan raised the technical achievement of the tall commercial building to the level of great architecture, but his voice was lost in the eclectic babel of the times. While the frenzied search for re-usable classical formulas and exotic ornament was pursued, the new building forms required by a radically changing industrial society came through industrial techniques. When sense and sensibility existed in the same man—for the 19th century succeeded in dividing these attributes as well—the structures of the engineers remain as the authentic works of architectural art; in other cases they are curious, but intensely meaningful documents of architectural advance.

One of the most remarkable agents of the architectural revolution wrought by the engineers was a new material: reinforced concrete. Even more than iron and steel, this material held the seeds of radical structure and style, made possible by properties unprecedented in the history of building. Its unparalleled strength, elasticity and plasticity and its unique monolithic nature were to lead to still another kind of construction —the enclosure of space with huge open spans, thin-shelled vaults, startling cantilevers and free-curving shapes impossible to the traditional post and beam or conventional metal girders. The brief history of contemporary reinforced concrete goes back to John Smeaton's rediscovery of the material in England in the 19th century (concrete was, of course, known to Rome, used most famously in the Pantheon dome), and the production of modern Portland cement in 1824. It progresses through English, French, German and American developments for the first three quarters of the century, in a confusion of discovery and re-discovery and conflicting claims; experiments took place independently and simultaneously on both sides of the Atlantic. Gardener Joseph Monier's famous application of wire netting reinforcement to concrete planting tubs was patented in France in 1867, but long before this date dusty patent office files contained a history of experiment and invention, rich with implication for the architectural forms of our time. Not until 1873 did Monier realize the far-reaching possibilities of his discovery, taking then additional patents to extend his system to reservoirs and bridges, from which a vast area of practical applications was pursued. After 1875 improvements in reinforced concrete were rapid and its use became widespread. In 1877, the American Thaddeus Hyatt published "An Account of Some Experiments with Portland Cement Concrete Combined with Iron as a Building Material with Reference to Economy in Construction and for Security Against Fire in the Making of Roofs, Floors and Walking Surfaces." From trials conducted for him in England, Hyatt stated specifically that bond existed between iron and concrete—a matter of considerable conjecture then and later—and that iron must resist sufficient tension stress to balance the compressive stresses in the concrete. His patent, taken out in 1878, was so broad in its coverage as to include most of the field of reinforced concrete construction. Shortly after, German engineers bought the rights to Monier's patents, and conducted a series of tests in the '80's that established the first scientific calculations for the strength of the material.

In the '90's the concrete age burst into full bloom. France took the lead as men like Coignet, Cottancin, Considère and Hennebique improved on previous construction and design. Although Cottancin's designs had a spectacular beauty prophetic of the new structural esthetic, his system, patented in 1889, did not lend itself to easy calculation, and François Hennebique may more properly be called the father of modern reinforced concrete construction. Hennebique's patent of 1892 covered a system of girders, beams and slabs, and the continuation of reinforcements from one member to another marking the beginnings of monolithic construction. Spurred by practical advantages—economy, fire-resistance and speed of erection—the use of reinforced concrete became general.

All this, however, was still classified as scientific, technological and utilitarian; it did not penetrate the realm of art. By 1900 the art world had a new enthusiasm—the flowing, plant-like forms of the linear, decorative movement known as *Art Nouveau.* While engineers like Hennebique built dams, bridges, warehouses and factories in Europe, and pioneers like Ernest Ransome developed even simpler and more economical reinforced concrete systems in the United States for the new mass-production plants of the expanding American economy, artists and architects, traveling another road in conscious pursuit of a new and different kind of design, treated themselves to the sinuous, "plaster pastry" of the 1900 Paris "macaroni" exhibition, so well described by Paul Morand. (The 1900 Exposition also exhibited the reinforced concrete skeletons of Coignet and Hennebique.) For the new engineering structures were still not looked upon as art, or as architecture. The unfamiliar forces of the material dictated unusual shapes and proportions which were considered practical, but inexcusably ugly. Accustomed to the massive solidity of load-bearing masonry columns and walls, critics rejected the light base of a three-hinged arch as unsubstantial and esthetically unsatisfactory. The complete readjustment of supports, loads and stresses required and made possible by reinforced concrete offended the tradition-trained eye. It remained for the 20th century to acquire an appreciative vision for these unorthodox effects. Today we evaluate them in their historical context—as the products of an industrial and technological revolution that profoundly influenced construction and produced a changing society with new building needs. Seen against this background, and against a concurrent 20th-century development—the evolution of a startling new esthetic that has changed the look of the world—contemporary reinforced concrete construction is understood as distinctly, magnificently and unequivocally of our own time. As a major achievement of modern building, it ranks with the most significant developments of the art of architecture. One of its most important figures and finest practitioners is the Italian engineer, Pier Luigi Nervi.

II

It is not as strange as it seems that one of the greatest builders of modern times is not an architect, but an engineer. Since structure is the basis of modern architecture (although many critics still labor under the delusion that it is possible to separate the skin—or look of a building—from its steel or concrete bones), it is scarcely surprising that an engineer of superior esthetic sensitivity has carried the new structural methods to a unique form of architectural realization. In view of the development just outlined, it is quite reasonable that the best contemporary architecture has grown out of great engineering, rather than the other way round.

Pier Luigi Nervi's importance lies in the fact that he has reunited architecture and engineering. His work re-establishes architecture as a primarily structural art, as it has always been in the best productive periods of the past. As such, Nervi's finest buildings are an incontrovertible fusion of science and art. They begin as structural concepts for a stated function, and are developed as sound solutions for specific needs. At the same time, they take forms of singular, and completely contemporary beauty. Because the nature of reinforced concrete construction makes structure and shape inseparable, and Nervi's sense of both is equally sound, the buildings have not only beauty, but truth. They are true to their purpose, their means, and their times. The richly decorative elements that add so much to the austere vocabulary of modern architecture—parabolic curves, lamella vaults, sunburst ceilings, ribbed roof slabs, fan-shaped buttresses, fluted shells—are the basic working parts as well as the ornamental delight of his designs. At no time is there any sense of arbitrary esthetic selection, or of *tour-de-force,* as is so often the case with his fellow architects, when they employ dramatic engineering devices. Even those of Nervi's designs that are not admirable in all of their aspects—there have been some questionable architectural collaborations and some less-than-distinguished exteriors—still have this remarkable structural "rightness," achieved with forms of exceptional power and grace, marking his personal style and making the building memorable. His feeling for form is as sure as his almost uncanny understanding of the complex structural possibilities of the material.

To achieve this, Nervi—a phenomenon in the modern world of specialization—became designer, calculator and constructor of his edifices, out of necessity—*per forza,* as the Italians say, because he had to; he alone was capable of conceiving them, and he found no one else capable of building them. His contracting firm, Nervi and

Bartoli, figures and bids on his own designs, many of which are the result of competitions, and carries out construction of these designs according to his own methods. Expertly trained technicians, carefully indoctrinated by Nervi himself, use construction techniques of his invention, undreamed of by conventional contractors. Craftsmanship, under his personal supervision, is in the finest Italian tradition. Translation of idea to actuality does not depend on less able, less imaginative engineers, nor is it affected by the builder's usual bias toward conservative solidity and the less-than-economical use of materials of a cost-plus operation. By functioning as a master-builder, in the past tradition of architecture, Nervi has been able to design unprecedented structures, and to devise unprecedented ways of building them.

That Nervi thinks of himself primarily as an architect, however, is obvious from his writings. "The proper title of a man capable of conceiving and building a structure is 'architect'," [4] he says, deploring the art-engineering split that still persists in architectural education and practice today. He urges the permanent healing of the breach between the two for a creative synthesis of structure and design. His most recent book sums up his philosophy in its two word title, *Costruire Correttamente*. [5] "To build correctly," he believes, is the essence of architecture; ". . . structural correctness . . . is identical with functional, technical and economic truthfulness and is a necessary and sufficient condition of satisfactory esthetic results." [6] Buildings conceived and executed in terms of "structure, function and economy" will always be creditable, and can, depending upon the capacity of the designer, "reach the superior heights of art."

Significantly, art, for Nervi, as for other master-builders of history, is an all-inclusive word. His definition of art expressed in a thoughtful treatise written during the late war years, *Scienza o Arte del Costruire?* ("Construction, Science or Art?")[7] goes far beyond esthetics to include intuitive, sensitive mastery of all of the incalculable elements of building in concrete. In this sense, the artistic process of designing a building involves creative judgment of many factors that expand and add to the traditional esthetic factors of proportion, chiaroscuro, color, surface and shape. This judgment is based on "static intuition," a kind of scientific sixth sense. Nervi buildings begin, not with formulas, but with a general concept, which he feels is spontaneous and partly subconscious, although it obviously rests on thorough structural knowledge. For, surprisingly, the use of reinforced concrete is still far from an exact science. Nervi makes the point over and over again that the mathematical calculations of the theory of structures (which he would prefer to call the mechanics of elastic systems) can be used only to analyze a structure already designed, and is of little assistance in the early creative stages. "The most advanced chapters of theory of structures, that deal with the solution of statically indeterminate systems, can be used only to check the stability of a structure . . . to analyze numerically a structure already designed, not only in its general outline, but in all its dimensional relations. The formative stage of a design, during which its main characteristics are defined and its qualities and faults are determined once and for all (just as the characteristics of an organism are clearly defined in the embryo) cannot make use of structural theory and must resort to intuitive and schematic simplification." [8] He feels that the value of intuition—in this day of almost religious reliance on mathematical formulas—cannot be overstressed, although this intuition must be based, not on esthetic *mystique,* but on a general mastery of our "new, most vast and difficult architectonic language, in all of its functional vocabulary —structural, technical and statical." [9] At the same time, he does not believe it necessary for the architect to be overtrained in specialized engineering knowledge. "If one considers that the architect must be first of all a conceiver of ideas, and successively the coordinator of the work of various specialists, one sees easily that he must have a synthesizing mentality and know the limitations and possibilities of every branch of structural techniques . . . he must have sufficient static intuition to nourish and guide his inventive fantasy and at the same time the mastery of a few simplified formulas . . . I think that all technical instruction in architecture should be essentially conceptual; specifics are quickly forgotten, and besides, are rapidly replaced by technical progress . . . the architect must not be a specialist in any technical branch, but must have clearer general ideas and concepts than all the specialists who are his collaborators . . . it is enough to have general knowledge, and a bit of good sense, to conserve the moral authority that an architect must always have with his associates . . . to keep the mastery of his work." [10]

A dedicated teacher, as well as a builder, he is saddened by the fact that the most admired student is the one who is most adept at mathematical theory. He is as much against the "formula designer" as against what the profession calls the "pretty picture school"—experts at the evocation of architectural irrelevancies through clever sketches and renderings. "Mathematics and drawing are means to be used in engineering and architecture, but they are not the whole of these disciplines, and if used incorrectly may even impair the clarity of a technical idea or the correctness of an architectural inspiration. . . ." [11] Patient and passionate work remain the architect's best tools.

Implicit in all of this, is Nervi's belief in the primary creativity of the architect, above and beyond the mechanics of the structural systems of which he must have full basic control. In his educational theory he advocates an architectural curriculum which places equal emphasis on esthetic and structural training. He has, however, even more practical reasons for stressing the role of intuition in building with reinforced concrete. The theory of structures, he claims, assumes ideal, perfect and constant conditions of a kind that never exist in nature. In reality, there are innumerable circumstances that affect a structure, of which abstract theory takes little note: building materials, particularly masonry and concrete, flow viscously; structures decay; soil settles unevenly; unpredictable daily weather changes take their toll; cements and limes continue to harden; all materials are slowly transformed. "Reinforced concrete presents hidden deficiencies and specific characteristics which make its structural behavior difficult, if not altogether impossible, to foresee exactly. Its high thermal sensitivity, its shrinkage, and above all, its plasticity . . . shatter our hope of investigating or knowing either before or after construction the real conditions of equilibrium of any statically indeterminate structure." [12]

In spite of these problems, modern reinforced concrete is one of the most rewarding and expressive of materials. Nervi's claim that it frees the structural imagination almost completely, suggests the unprecedented architectural avenues that it opens. Because it is the nature of man—and of the architect—to cling to accustomed patterns, there has always been a tendency to use new materials in old ways, often more suitable to traditional processes and needs, so that the value of intuition and imagination in the development of reinforced concrete architecture cannot be underestimated. Nervi has lacked neither. Although he modestly attributes all of his contributions to simple logic and common sense, they are the expression of a brilliant technical mind, unhampered by conventional attitudes, exploring without prejudice the potential of a still unknown material.

Working first with conventional reinforced concrete, his experience with the obvious fact that concrete withstands large strains best in the areas of reinforcement and that the distribution and subdivision of reinforcement affects the strength of the material, led to his development of a revolutionary kind of reinforced concrete: "Ferro-cemento." Ferro-cemento is a thin, flexible, elastic and very strong material composed of several layers of fine steel mesh—ductile steel wire 0.02 to 0.06 inches in diameter, set 0.4 inches apart—sprayed with cement mortar; the total thickness of the slab little greater than the bulk of the mesh. For heavier construction, reinforcing rods are inserted in the center of a sandwich of layers of mortar and mesh. The advantages over ordinary reinforced concrete are considerable. As Nervi has pointed out in teaching, experiment and actual construction, Ferro-cemento can stand great strains without cracking, and because of its superior strength and elasticity can be used in exceedingly thin slabs and shells. In many instances formwork can be avoided because the cement mortar can be applied directly to the shaped mesh, as plaster is to metal lath. Beyond its use for building, Nervi favors Ferro-cemento as a natural material for ship design and has demonstrated its efficacy for strong, thin boat shells.

Besides the development of a new material, Nervi has made another, equally revolutionary advance: the elimination of wooden forms, and with them, the restrictions that rectilinear wood planks have always imposed on the shape and style of reinforced concrete structures. First, through Ferro-cemento, it is possible to prefabricate parts, even without forms, for later site-erection. Second, by making the necessary forms in Ferro-cemento, any desirable shape can be obtained,—free, curving ribs or undulating corrugated slabs of superb structural efficiency, relating directly to the static forces of complex structures by directly following the main lines of stress. The use of plaster molds for Ferro-cemento forms also results in clean, smooth surfaces, requiring no additional finishing. A case in point is the reticulated network of the Gatti wool factory ceilings (plates 55–57) in Rome, where Nervi's associate, Aldo Arcangeli, devised a system based on the principle of having the ribs of the slab follow the isostatic lines of its principal bending moments for an effect of natural organic grace that is an unwitting fulfillment of Alberti's 15th-century description of nerved netted vaults.[13] The parallel is purely visual (and esthetic), for the physical principles were then unknown. Nervi's radical work with prefabricated parts proved that the monolithic qualities that are both the nature and advantage of concrete construction were not disturbed by breaking the structure down into precast elements. This truth was tragically, but satisfactorily demonstrated when the Germans dynamited his airplane hangars after the war. Although they lay shattered on the ground, the joints between prefabricated elements were still found to be intact.

This free prefabrication of parts and consequent expansion of usable structural shapes changes the whole concept of reinforced concrete construction. Today's design is a far cry from earlier buildings, limited to poured-in-place structures with some simple, prefabricated members, all based on the use of rigidly rectangular wooden forms. Forms for less conservative shapes were built with great difficulty and expense. Nervi's development of structural prefabrication and re-usable Ferro-cemento forms on movable scaffolding have not only broadened the range of reinforced concrete design, but have also made possible the speedy, economical and accurate erection of large factories and industrial installations like the 1952 tobacco factory at Bologna, (plates 49–54) and the 1955 Turin Fiat plant (plates 70–75).

In addition, these technical innovations have introduced a radical new vocabulary of forms to the art of architecture. As the structural concepts and techniques change—due largely to Nervi's novel procedures—appearance is also transformed. His methods offer the possibility of an unlimited exploration of three-dimensional shapes in building. Only his fellow engineers—Torroja in Spain, Candela in Mexico, Maillart in Switzerland, Freyssinet in France—have demonstrated a similar capacity for the creation of engineering works of art. Conviction, strength and correctness make these buildings architectonic statements of particular significance for our age.

III

NERVI'S contributions are particularly impressive measured against the background of his education and his times. His professional training—he was graduated from the Civil Engineering School of Bologna in 1913—was in the formal "art versus science" tradition of the day. His future role, as a man who was to question these ideals, find them unrealistic and denounce them for an entirely new concept of building is all the more remarkable in view of his solid indoctrination in the Victorian architectural philosophy already described. "When I studied at the excellent Civil Engineering School at Bologna, the word architecture referred only to the study of facades and of their details. It never occurred to our professors, or even to us, that a bridge, a carrying structure, an urban plan, could also be works of architecture. . . . Structures in reinforced concrete or iron, in spite of already existing examples of great bridges, of the Eiffel tower, were considered technical feats developed in fields that had nothing to do with architecture. . . . I remember many examples seen during that period—at exhibitions of the new architecture—a church project, for example, with a *pronaos* [portico] held up by pilasters so tall and thin that it would have been absolutely impossible to have executed it even in welded steel. . . ." These designs were more concerned with the look of a building than how it was put together, an approach based on a false formalism that emphasized "the division between substance and appearance . . . the mentality of the decorator, to which everything is possible in the field of mouldings and plastic and pictorial decoration . . . ignorance of the physical entity of architecture, which, like a living being, cannot separate beauty from the physiological health of the body." [14]

At the same time that academic dogma clung to these outmoded ideals, they were being shattered by contemporary practice. Nervi relates, in *Costruire Correttamente,* how his professor of structure (one of the few theoreticians aware of the limitations of the theories he taught) read letters of German engineers who predicted, on the basis of mathematical calculations, that Hennebique's Risorgimento Bridge in Rome, built in 1913, could not possibly stand although it was already completed and in use. This important construction, and other trend-setting achievements of the same years, were ignored by the schools and the architectural profession. Although Nervi stated that he was not aware of much of the pioneering work then in process until many years later, reinforced concrete had come into its full majority in the first decade of the new century. Hennebique's exceptional talent as a businessman and promoter, in addition to his outstanding abilities as an engineer, resulted in widespread publicity and universal use for the new material. As early as 1903, Auguste Perret had established concrete architecturally in his famous Paris apartment house at 25 *bis* Rue Franklin, a landmark of the modern movement notable for its cantilevered construction and exposed concrete frame. By 1907, the Queen Alexandria Sanatorium had been built in Davos, Switzerland, by architects Pfleghard and Haefeli, with the engineer, Robert Maillart, collaborating. Maillart's slim, economical concrete bridges crossed Switzerland's lesser-known valleys as early as 1900; his shallow, curved-slab Tavanasa span of 1905 set the standard of unsurpassed efficiency and artistry that was to distinguish his bridge designs through the 1930's. In 1910, his Zurich warehouse introduced the beamless mushroom ceiling to European design. Tony Garnier began his *"grand travaux"* for the city of Lyons in 1909, based on a highly original scheme of 1901–04 for a Cité Industrielle of reinforced concrete. In America, Ernest Ransome had constructed sizable reinforced concrete plants for the United Shoe Machinery Company in Beverly, Massachusetts in 1903–04, and the Foster-Armstrong Piano Company at Rochester, New York in 1904–05;[15] followed immediately by Albert Kahn's better known factories for the automobile industry. Reinforced concrete was in great demand for industrial and commercial building of all sorts; pre-cast "unit" systems had been widely patented and were in general use by 1910.[16]

In addition to the new structure, there was a significant stirring of new ideas about design. Architect Peter Behrens, in his 1909 Turbine Factory in Berlin, set an early standard for the frank visual expression of industrial architecture founded on engineering techniques. Walter Gropius' Fagus factory, which followed in 1911, was an even clearer indication of the coming industrial esthetic, which began with such utilitarian structures and eventually spread to every field of building design. The establishment of the Deutsche Werkbund of 1907 marked the practical beginnings of collaboration between art and industry, a significant forerunner of the post-World War One Bauhaus movement which was to be so immensely influential in establishing the machine esthetic internationally. All of this was to lead to the acceptance of the undisguised engineering structure of the new architectural technology as the reasonable basis of a radical and unfamiliar beauty. The world was on the way to a "new look."

Nervi's own development was undoubtedly made possible by the rising tide of the modern movement, to which he, in turn, made conspicuous contributions. He tells of this himself: "When I began my constructing activity, the technical problems connected with architecture were very modest: open spans of ten to fifteen metres were, in fact, exceptional, coverings of fifteen to twenty metres, truly audacious. . . . Year by year I have seen the growth not only of the complexity of static problems, and of those deriving from improving technical equipment, but above all I have seen the growth of the size and impressiveness of bearing structures to the point when they have become so remarkable that they can never again be lost under traditional . . . decorations . . . and trimmings. . . . A real revolution was being confirmed: the great majority of those concerned with architecture, professionally and culturally, agreed that even a bare, sincere structure could give the full effect of beauty and could be true architecture, and that, on the other hand, forms and volumes, set by technical and functional necessity, treated with sensibility, could become eloquent means of architectonic expression. . . . Today no one doubts that a work of architecture must be a stable, unified, enduring organism, in accordance with its surroundings and the functions that it must satisfy, balanced in all of its parts, sincere in its supporting structure and technical elements, and at the same time capable of giving that indefinable emotion that we call beauty . . . and that this result can be achieved with a liberty of means unsuspected yesterday."[17]

This dual revolution—structural and esthetic—is clearly illustrated in the development of Nervi's work. After graduation, approximately ten years with the Società per Costruzioni Cementizie (interrupted from 1915 to 1918 by the war) provided invaluable experience with one of the best organizations in Italy engaged in reinforced concrete work. To this experience, in Bologna before the war, and in Florence after, Nervi attributes important formative influences, technically and structurally. Although Freyssinet's trend-setting parabolic hangars were built at Orly in 1916, followed by the Bagneux locomotive sheds in 1929, he claims that it was not until the late '30's that he became fully aware of the experiments of Perret, Maillart, Freyssinet and others, and that his own personal expression developed partly through this cultural isolation, which he considers a peculiarly advantageous, if not particularly praiseworthy circumstance, since he approached new problems without benefit of examples or preconceived ideas. Then as now, his primary concern was with technical, economical and functional requirements, which he attempted to solve in the best possible manner, through painstaking and exhaustive research. "The thought never passed through my mind to question how others had, or might have, solved similar problems." [18]

In 1920, he formed his own firm—Soc. Ing. Nervi e Nebbiosi—in Rome, a collaboration that lasted until 1932. Under these independent auspices, a limited number of startling buildings began to appear. (A complete list of Nervi's work will be found on pp. 113, 114. Only the most important executed projects will be discussed here, and whenever possible, descriptions will be in Nervi's own words.[19])

The first of these buildings was the small Cinema Augusteo in Naples, in 1926–27. It was followed by the Municipal Stadium of Florence, begun in 1929 and completed, after an interruption of work, in 1932, a structure that immediately attracted international attention (plates 1–6). Like almost all of Nervi's works, the commission was won as the result of a competition, and the design was selected largely for its extraordinary economy. (The cost averaged $2.90 a seat, for a stadium of 35,000 seats.) The terraced steps that form the seats act as structural beams, buttressed from below, with expansion joints at 100 foot intervals. An oval shape and asymmetrical layout was necessitated by a 657 foot running track in front of the covered grandstand. This grandstand is one of the structure's outstanding features. The roof is a shell stiffened by cantilevered curved beams on 15 foot 6 inch centers, with expansion joints at every third beam. Forces from the cantilever are distributed through a fork-shaped construction stiffened by horizontal beams, to supporting columns 52 feet high. The springing, graceful roof demonstrates Nervi's structural clarity: the thick-and-thin shape of the roof trusses indicates the points of chief concentration of forces, providing at the same time a dramatically powerful form. Nervi explains the determinants of the design: "The variation in section of the main ribs is dictated by the law governing the variation of moments. Purely esthetic considerations inspired the slight curve of the canopy and the haunching of the main ribs."

The exterior stairs, (plate 1) five 10-foot wide, exposed helicoidal spirals, add a visual and structural accent not unlike sculptural abstraction. "An interesting problem was set by these outside staircases," Nervi relates, "which involved considerable difficulties in construction, and which made me realize, for the first time, the extent to which the full development of reinforced concrete is linked up with the problem of timber formwork and its inability to adapt itself to curving or spiralling surfaces. I found the exact calculation of staircases impossible, and I therefore limited myself to a calculation of this complex, statically indeterminate system in terms of simple, statically determinate elements, and calculated them for the greatest stability even at the cost of high unit stresses, as I was confident that the wonderful plastic qualities of concrete would of themselves bring about full and efficient monolithicity between the structural elements. Events have fully justified my confidence, and the strictest application tests and—more important—time and use have demonstrated the perfect stability of the structure."

The main facade behind the covered tribunal and the interior court of honor were architectural flourishes executed in the typical arid neo-classicism of the official fascist style of the '30's. These less-than-desirable features, however, are overpowered, and even cancelled out by the strength and originality of the main design.

In 1932 Nervi became associated with a cousin to form the design and construction firm, Ingg. Nervi e Bartoli, which he has headed to the present day. In 1938, the new firm undertook the engineering of a series of airplane hangars that were to be landmarks in the development of reinforced concrete construction (plates 7–13). A competition organized by the Italian air force authorities in 1935 called for several large hangars, spanning 330 feet by 135 feet internally, with door openings of 165 feet. Again, Nervi was awarded the contract, and his solutions, as usual, were conspicuously economical and easy to erect. They used concrete ingeniously in a country where steel is traditionally scarce, and labor plentiful. These hangars had a structural magnificence infrequently achieved, and seldom equalled. "I designed the structure as a geodetic framework acting together as a whole, as I believed this would give the most economical solution and the one requiring the least steel. With this type of design the theoretical calculations were extremely complicated. . . . I therefore decided to make a preliminary calculation and then to make a detailed study of the stresses by means of experiments on a model. . . . I believe that this is one of the first instances in which the results of model tests have been applied to a really large-scale structure. The results of the model tests enabled me to go fully into the static behaviour of the structure and to estimate the stresses in the whole framework, and it was found that the preliminary estimates provided by the preliminary calculations used in the construction of the model required hardly any alteration. The actual construction was not easy, and provided yet another illustration of the economic disadvantages of timber formwork wherever reinforced concrete work goes beyond the simplest shapes."

To overcome these disadvantages, Nervi developed a second design in 1940 (plates 12–13). The first version was a space-spanning lamella vault, with poured-in-place concrete beams and ribs, roofed with hollow tile, supported by five large and twenty-one small buttresses. The front edge of the roof was stiffened along its greatest opening by a box girder. Wherever the ribs crossed, they were welded and grouted. This painstaking joining, arduous formwork, and *in situ* pouring, were all laborious operations.

In the second type, Nervi attempted to speed up the process by the development of prefabricated parts. "At that time, the need for economy in materials and timber had become even more acute and this is why, on the basis of the experience acquired, I decided to simplify and lighten the structure by designing the ribs as a lattice, which would enable me to make use of prefabrication. I also altered the system of supports in order to simplify the static system and make it more symmetrical." Rather than build complete forms for pouring the structure, he used these precast, open girders, assembling them aloft, for a huge, lacy, vaulted structure, thirty feet high, carried by only six supports. The effect, particularly before roofing in, was of incredible lightness and strength. Further support was provided by box girders around the entire outer edge, and poured-in-place solid beams at the points of greatest stress. Again, the work was unprecedented and model tests were necessary. "The greater structural simplicity and the extensive study made of the previous hangar design enabled me to make a still better approximate calculation, the results of which agreed exactly with those of the model tests. The precasting of the units and their erection proved quite simple. The joints were made by welding the steel and placing high strength concrete in the space left at the junction of four units. The results were excellent, as may be observed on visiting the remains of the six hangars. The Germans destroyed them when they retreated by demolishing the supporting columns, but even after the fall of the roof, the great majority of the joints are still intact." About a dozen hangars of both types were built at Orvieto, Orbetello, Torre del Lago, and other sites, from 1937 to 1943.

In the mid-forties Nervi developed Ferro-cemento, his own versatile variation of reinforced concrete (see page 19) that was to make still further design and structural innovations possible. The outstanding result was the grand "Salone B" of the Turin Exposition Hall of 1948–49 (plates 24–36), one of the most impressive interior spaces of this century. If ever economy has spurred art, Nervi's work is a prime example. Once more, a remarkable solution was chosen largely for its low cost. Submitted as a competition entry, it offered the cheapest and quickest replacement for an exhibition hall destroyed during the war.[20] This extraordinary interior opened the eyes of the world to a new kind of architectural space. Roofed by an undulating, corrugated vault, the lines of force arching across the ceiling are gathered into fan-shaped buttresses at the sides of the hall, and transmitted to underground supports. The bare display of structure and the calculated beauty of the structural forms is literally stunning. To Nervi, it was a chance to prove his theories in practical fashion. "The problem was particularly interesting, not only because of the dimensions of the hall (nearly 330 foot span) but also because of the very short time allowed for the execution of the work, which was to start in September and had to be finished by the end of April. This very short time was a real problem in view of the difficult climate in Turin. The solution I immediately thought of was a structure in corrugated Ferro-cemento, which would attain the necessary stability by virtue of the corrugations and would enable us to use precasting, and to manufacture the roof units while the floors and supporting structure were being built. On this basis I designed a roof structure with corrugations of about 8 foot span, divided into units 13 feet long. The units were to be made of Ferro-cemento in order to be as light as possible (thickness 1½ inches) and would be rendered monolithic by reinforced concrete ribs cast in place, and located at the peaks and troughs of the corrugations. In this way the Ferro-cemento units would act as junction units between the *in situ* ribs which in turn would take over the main structural work. The units are closed at each end by stiffening diaphragms and adjacent units are joined together by a 1½ inch thickness of mortar."

"The casting of the ribs proceeded without any difficulty and without the need for double formwork, as would have been the case with ordinary reinforced concrete. . . . Lifting and placing the units proceeded regularly (the units were unmoulded in two or three days) and enabled about 3,230 square feet of roof to be completed each day. The construction took place in three stages, to get the fullest possible use from the movable formwork. The corrugated roof was connected to the main supporting columns (which are at 24 foot 7½ inch centres) by fan-shaped Ferro-cemento units springing from inclined reinforced concrete elements."

For the design of the 130 foot diameter half-dome at the end of the main Exhibition Hall Nervi introduced a new kind of prefabrication (plates 30, 31). "I used a method based on precast units, which I had studied and actually used, though on small-scale structures, immediately after the war. This method had also been inspired by the need for economizing in timber, which was extremely scarce in Italy at that time. The method is suitable for the construction of vaults or domes and consists of filling the space to be covered with precast units measuring approximately 6 feet 6 inches by 13 feet. The units are cast in concrete molds which in turn are constructed on a model reproducing a section of the vault or dome to be built. The edges of each unit are so shaped that when placed side by side they form channels about 4 inches wide between the units, which are filled with reinforced concrete and form a network of supporting ribs that complete the structural system. The units are made of Ferro-cemento and are ¾ of an inch thick. During erection they are supported on scaffolding and require no actual formwork. The units may be made in any shape and, provided allowance is made for the formation of the ribs, they lend themselves readily to the expression of any architectural form."

The one jarring element in the superb rhythmic harmony of the design is the connection between the half-dome and the main hall. As originally proposed by Nervi, a curved-glass division separated the two, and the supports followed the same strong diagonals that indicated the direction of forces throughout. As executed, it rests on a dull series of ordinary columns in fancy-dress marble facing—a prosaic, rectilinear arrangement that conceals and denies the dynamics of the structure.

One year later, a second hall was built: "Salone C," measuring 180 feet by 540 feet (plates 37–42). "Again, the time allowed for completion was very short, as the work was to be started in November, and had to be ready before the end of March. It was again necessary to use precasting, which could conveniently be carried out in the basement of the adjoining main hall. My design was for a hipped vault, supported by four arches on a sloping plane with a slope corresponding approximately to the thrust of the vault. For the construction of the vault, I decided to use the same method as for the half-dome in the main exhibition building, covering the required area with precast units placed in rows parallel to the angles of the roof and allowing for a strip of glazing around the edges to provide daylighting. To obtain this daylighting, the units in this part of the roof consisted only of the channels which formed the ribs. For the surrounding flat-roofed portion, which spans 33 feet, I designed a system of corrugated beams in Ferro-cemento, precast at the same time as the vault units. These beams, ¾ of an inch thick at the top, increasing to 1½ inches at the soffit to provide room for the necessary reinforcement, are placed side by side and finished with a lightweight screed. Erection proved very quick and easy. The beams were cast in concrete molds which, in turn, had been made in a plaster mold. The visible underside of the beam, which is in contact with the form during casting, is regular and smooth, with a perfection of surface that could never be obtained by any of the usual finishing processes. This method of construction is very adaptable; I have used it many times for curved structures, and always with excellent results."

A series of domes, vaults and ceilings in the next few years repeated this same system with interesting variations: the Beach Casino at Ostia, 1950 (with architect Attilio La Padula); the elliptical roof of the hall at the Terme di Chiancino, 1952 (with architects Mario Loreti and Mario Marchi); (plates 46–48) the parabolic vault of the Tortona Salt Warehouse, 1950–51; (plates 44, 45) the Municipal Tramway Depot in Turin, 1954 (plates 60–62).

For a competition held by the State Monopoly Administration in 1949, requiring a design for a five story, 700' x 80' x 90' factory, Nervi devised a new method of constructing roofs, used in the Tobacco Factory at Bologna, in 1952 (plates 49–54), and for the exceptionally long (2100 feet) Turin Fiat Works in 1955 (plates 70–75). Re-usable Ferro-cemento molds, mounted on travelling scaffolding, moving both horizontally and vertically, eliminate all of the traditional restrictions of timber framework. Columns are built up first, then the ceiling is cast, one bay at a time, the molds lowered, moved on, jacked into position, and reused for each succeeding bay.

"This new freedom," Nervi points out, "also made it possible to design roofs with ribs located along the isostatic lines of the principle bending moments, a design which makes possible strict adherence to the laws of statics and, therefore, makes the most efficient use of the materials." A particularly effective example of this is the Gatti wool factory ceiling in Rome, of 1953 (plates 55–57), a direct reflection of the scientific laws of structure. Nor is Nervi unaware of the sensuous implications of this kind of engineering. "The esthetically satisfying result of the interplay of ribs placed in this way is a clear reminder of the mysterious affinity to be found between physical laws and our own senses."

Some of Nervi's buildings are more ambitious projects than the utilitarian ones on which his reputation rests. There are important international edifices, designed in collaboration with major architects: UNESCO Headquarters in Paris (plates 78–95), completed in 1957, with Marcel Breuer and Bernard H. Zehrfuss; and the Pirelli Building in Milan (plates 98–101), with architects Gio Ponti, Alberto Rosselli, and an impressive number of distinguished engineering colleagues. In these architectural collaborations, however, a curious situation arises. In spite of august names and high objectives, these buildings frequently fall short of Nervi's finest expression alone. His own work is concerned primarily with the search for correct structural solutions for utilitarian problems. The plain, unpretentious factory exteriors that often cloak the elegance of his structural systems may not be overly distinguished, but they have dignity and suitability. They want no dressing up. His best buildings are directly functional, and achieve their decorative and sculptural qualities as a natural by-product of their techniques. Almost invariably, they come off considerably better than those designs in which his structural innovations are incorporated into more self-consciously architectural schemes. In these more ambitious projects, structure becomes sophisticated play, as in the folded roof and walls of the UNESCO conference building, or turns into an arbitrary and ultimately questionable technique for an equally questionable unconventionality, as in the Pirelli skyscraper. Quite often, as in the Pirelli building, the engineering forms, magnificent in themselves, are eventually covered by a far less expressive, architect-designed skin. Usually, there is a strong suggestion of calculated selection of structural forms, rather than Nervi's customary single-minded concentration on "the most efficient design from the technical and economic point of view" . . . "free from existing esthetic theories." [21] The few times in the past that he has kept one eye cocked for architectural effect, the results have been disastrous. He denounces these indiscretions himself: "Because of flattering comment . . . I tried to bring esthetic theories to bear upon structural problems . . . but soon convinced myself that to find an architectonic expression becomes more difficult the more one works with such an idea in mind."

Unfortunately, the architects who work with Nervi are seldom as directly concerned as he is with the primacy of the structural solution. They admire it, and desire it, but they are equally anxious about its esthetic effect, and preoccupied with the necessity of "making an architectural statement." They are no longer concerned first with solving problems; their intent is to create architecture. This conscious effort stamps the structure with an unmistakable look of calculated cleverness. It has become structure for art's sake. For the most serious foe of architecture is the man who sets out deliberately to produce it.

In spite of its disappointments, however, the UNESCO building represents a capable and conscientious collaboration. If the effects appear somewhat arbitrary, they do not depart from legitimate reinforced concrete engineering. The roof and end wall of the Conference Building (plates 90–95) demonstrate the ingenious use of a folded concrete slab, its shape determined by the compressive forces of the roof structure. The Y-shaped Secretariat is raised on massive concrete supports (plates 83, 84); canopies (plates 86–88) exploit the material's plastic qualities. Nevertheless, the building lacks the vigorous sense of Nervi's structural directness, the reflection of his unshakeable faith in "... the prime condition of architectural expression ... the inevitability of its structural design." [22]

This expression of architectonic structure is far more evident in the sports buildings executed in Rome for the 1960 Olympics (plates 103–126). This problem, of course, permits more exposed structure and less architectural dressing-up: arenas and stadia are engineering problems before they are anything else, since the requirements of open span shells and amphitheatres call for special—and dominating—structural design. There are three buildings—a small, covered Palazzetto dello Sport, designed by Nervi with architect Annibale Vitellozzi, a larger, covered Palazzo dello Sport, with architect Marcello Piacentini; and the Stadio Flaminio, a 50,000 seat stadium designed with his son, Antonio.

Here there are no inert masses of masonry, or delicate games of design. Every part of the edifice makes a statement of purpose, translated into form. The flute-edged roof shell of the "Little Palace" (plate 106) is composed of prefabricated, diamond-shaped sections, joined by poured-in-place concrete that makes their connecting ribs, creating a webbed ceiling network of flowerlike elegance. A compression ring in the center forms a cupola, providing a central source of natural light. The forces that flow through these ribs are gathered in prefabricated, triangular sections, which transfer the load—carried outward and downward—to exterior Y-shaped buttresses and vertical supports. The building seats 5000.

The larger palace, seating 16,000, employs a similar system, of more intricate design. The ceiling sections, also prefabricated, follow the precedent of the Turin Exposition Hall, the units forming ribs that curve outward to the building's perimeter, held centrally by a tension ring. The prefabricated sections are joined by *in situ* pouring at their top and bottom points. From the exterior, however, the effect is considerably weaker than in the smaller building. Much of the interesting supporting structure is hidden by a glass-enclosed gallery wrapped around the main structure, connected to it by a canti-levered roof. The effect from the outside is of an almost neo-classic blandness that conveys little visual excitement. In contrast, the interior offers unparalleled drama. The forces of the ribbed ceiling are transmitted through prefabricated triangular sections to 48 joints resting on the 300 foot ring that is the upper edge of the seating section. This upper seating section is supported by poured-in-place columns (cast in movable, re-usable molds) with warped surfaces; the combination of their angular geometry with the reticulated under surface of the seating section is one of the build-ing's most striking effects.

The 460 by 590 foot stadium (plates 118–126) has a poured-in-place frame and prefabricated seats. The frame consists of ribs like those of a ship, with the seat struc-ture laid across them. The covered portion adds a cantilevered canopy, its weight resting on the upper ends of the ribs, assisted by diagonal braces at its central point. The canopy has its largest cross section at this point, tapering front and back. In section, both the frame and superstructure are shaped with noteworthy elegance.

These buildings, and all of Nervi's work, represent more than a structural revolution.

They also demonstrate the radical change in esthetic vision characteristic of all of the arts of our time.[23] Today, painting, sculpture, architecture, and the arts of design pursue weightlessness, forms in tension, and dynamic plastic expression, rather than the solidity and classic balance admired by earlier generations. A sympathy for solidity was natural in a world built of brick on brick and stone on stone; a preoccupation with lightness, dematerialization and dynamic forms in equilibrium is natural in a world of spider-strong steel, thin shell concrete, and amorphous plastics that invite new principles of construction and manufacture and the use of stimulating new shapes. New materials, new purposes, and new forms go hand in hand.

Nor is it a coincidence that the shapes of modern structural architecture restate the shapes of modern painting and sculpture. It is a truth, not a cliché, that there is a visual "language" for every age, spoken by all of its artists. We see this with particular effect in the architecture, painting and sculpture of classicism, of the baroque and the rococo, and we have developed a unique expression of it in our own time, with the aid of a technological revolution that has made this visual revolution possible in the practical building and industrial arts as well as in the less restricted fields of artistic experimentation. It is as a leader in these areas that Nervi's importance lies. He is a form-giver: his structural innovations have made it possible to develop those shapes in architecture with which we are in particular sympathy today.

However, if he is a form-giver, others are form-borrowers. Because the significance of his contribution is universally recognized, it is also universally imitated. Although its appearance, and even its ingenuity can be copied, its meaning is in the appropriateness of each individual solution for its specific purpose. It does not lend itself to general application. Attracted by its striking and unconventional aspect, intrigued by the possibilities of sensuous departures in modern design, architects are increasingly imitating the letter, but not the spirit of his production. Nervi, himself, is aware of this, and concerned. "The present moment in architecture is full of promise, but the dangers should not be overlooked. Alarming symptoms can already be seen. . . . Too often, through a lack of understanding of its structural and constructional *essence,* a structure is considered solely on the basis of its external appearance—which people try to adapt to a variety of different problems. . . . The result is always unfortunate . . . structural acrobatics are a sign of a false structural conception. . . . The fact is that it is easy to adhere superficially to new ideas, but it is very difficult to fully understand their substance. . . ." [23]

This copying of external appearances with flagrant disregard for their reason for being, Nervi calls "formalism,"—the same attitude that undermined creative architecture in the 19th-century. Still a threat today, ". . . its influence is particularly damaging in one of the most important, growing technical and architectonic fields—that of structural design. Structural architecture does not permit arbitrary or formal solutions, although—from the purely technical point of view—the constantly growing mechanical properties of materials and the accuracy of methods of calculation make them possible, even if they are achieved through a striking sacrifice of money, artificial solutions,

30

or abstract intellectual inspirations. . . . I have thought much about it, and I believe that I can affirm that an *architectonic* structure must be born and derived spontaneously from the 'static sense' that progress in engineering has in part brought about, sustaining and integrating it with the formal reasoning of the science of construction." [24]

In this new architecture, the static sense and the esthetic sense play an equal part. For even engineering based on structural necessity has its areas of free selection; form does not follow function without any factor of free esthetic choice. There is always more than one way to solve a problem. The difference between these solutions and the countless pragmatic structures serving similar purposes without distinction is the taut equilibrium and sensuous beauty of Nervi's personal poetry of structure. In the Italian architectural vocabulary, the word *poetica* is justified for his work alone.

The Notes to the Text begin on p. 113.

The Municipal Stadium of Florence, 1930–32. Stair to the grandstand.

2. The Municipal Stadium. View of the stadium.

3. The Municipal Stadium. Plan.

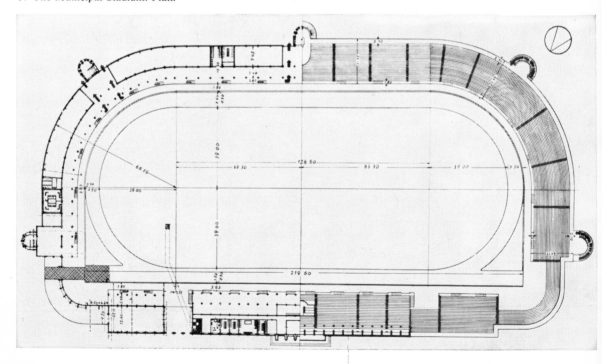

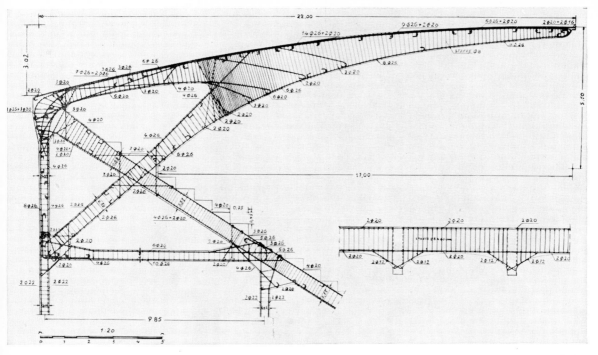

4. The Municipal Stadium. Section of the cantilevered frame suporting the roof of the covered grandstand showing reinforcing.

5. The Municipal Stadium. Covered grandstand.

6. The Municipal Stadium. Covered grandstand in construction, with supporting members still exposed.

7. Hangar, 1935. 328′ x 131′ x 26′.

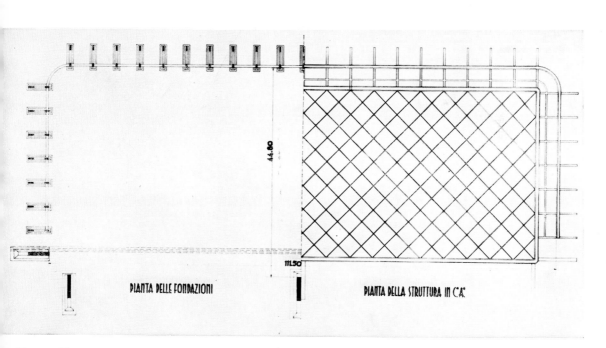

PIANTA DELLE FONDAZIONI

PIANTA DELLA STRUTTURA IN C.A.

8. Hangar. Plan.

9. Hangar. Detail of roof during construction: wooden frames for pouring concrete beams.

10. Hangar. Completed interior.

1. Hangar. Corner detail: buttresses and supporting beams of door.

12. Hangar, 1940. 328' x 131' x 39'. Skeleton of prefabricated concrete beams.

13. Hangar. Completed interior.

14. Underground storage tanks for gasoline, 1937. 54′ high, 101′ in diameter.

15. Underground storage tanks. Model.

16. Warehouse, Rome, 1945. Walls of Ferro-cemento, $1\frac{3}{16}''$ thick.

17. Swimming pool for the Naval Academy, Leghorn, 1947–49. Pre-fabricated ribs form the corrugated roof.

18. Swimming pool. In construction: setting prefabricated rib in place.

19, 20. Conte Trossi Wharf, San Michele di Pagano, Genoa, 1947. Designed with architect Luigi Carlo Daneri. Five reenforced concrete arches on 32′ centers span approximately 100′ to 115′; ceiling of precast, corrugated roof beams.

21. Project for 660' span, 1943. Prefabricated, truss-like elements.

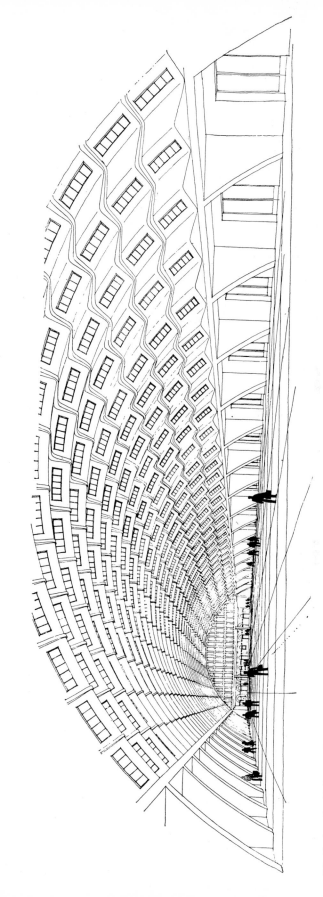

22. Project for Palermo Central Station, 1946. Roof of prefabricated units, similar to those used for the Turien Exposition Hall.

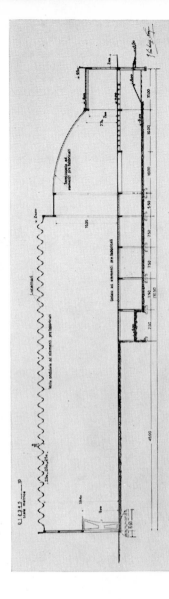

24. Exhibition Building, Turin, Salone B, 1948–49. Longitudinal section.

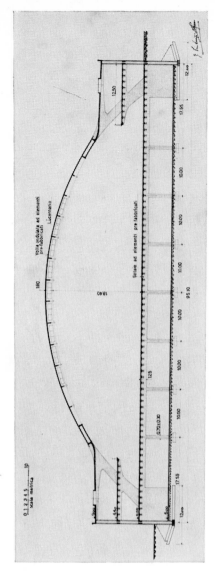

25. Exhibition Building, Salone B. Transverse section.

23. Exhibition Building, Turin, 1948–50. Plan.

26. Exhibition Building, Salone B.

27. Exhibition Building, Salone B. 243′ x 310′.

28. Exhibition Building, Salone B. Closeup of ceiling during construction.

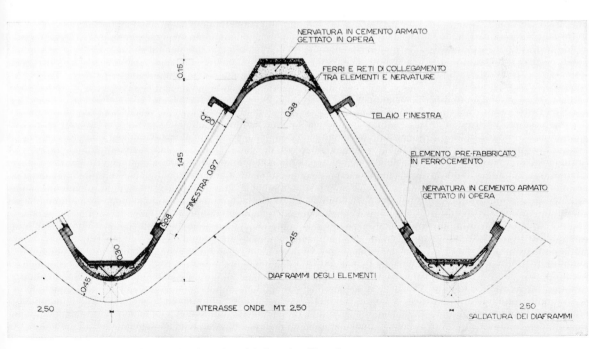

NERVATURA IN CEMENTO ARMATO
GETTATO IN OPERA

FERRI E RETI DI COLLEGAMENTO
TRA ELEMENTI E NERVATURE

TELAIO FINESTRA

ELEMENTO PRE-FABBRICATO
IN FERROCEMENTO

NERVATURA IN CEMENTO ARMATO
GETTATO IN OPERA

DIAFRAMMI DEGLI ELEMENTI

2,50

INTERASSE ONDE MT 2,50

2,50

SALDATURA DEI DIAFRAMMI

FINESTRA 0,97

0,15

0,38

0,20

1,45

0,08

0,45

0,30

0,45

29. Exhibition Building, Salone B. Section of prefabricated ceiling element.

30. Exhibition Building, Salone B. Construction of semi-cupola at end of Salone B; diameter 131′.

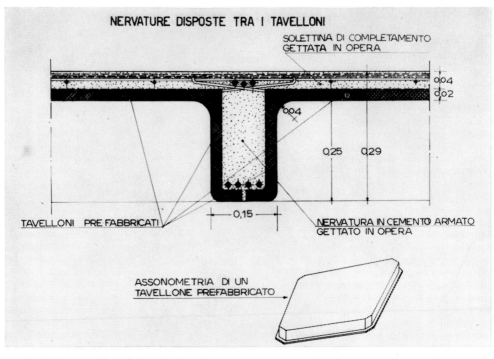

NERVATURE DISPOSTE TRA I TAVELLONI

SOLETTINA DI COMPLETAMENTO
GETTATA IN OPERA

0.04
0.02

0.04

0.25   0.29

0.15

TAVELLONI PRE FABBRICATI

NERVATURA IN CEMENTO ARMATO
GETTATO IN OPERA

ASSONOMETRIA DI UN
TAVELLONE PREFABBRICATO

31. Exhibition Building, Salone B. Detail of construction: prefabricated pan, and section showing
placing of pans and pouring of concrete network uniting them.

32. Exhibition Building, Salone B. In construction: movable scaffolding.

33. Exhibition Building, Salone B. Prefabricated ceiling units on ground.

34. Exhibition Building, Salone B. Prefabricated ceiling units of the arched ribs in place, joined by concrete poured along their summit and base.

35. Exhibition Building, Salone B. Ceiling ribs at their point of juncture, with fan-shaped units leading to buttresses building's sides.

36. Exhibition Building, Salone B. Completed interior showing same detail.

37. Exhibition Building, Turin, Salone C, 1949–50. Approximately 165′ x 215′ x 45′.

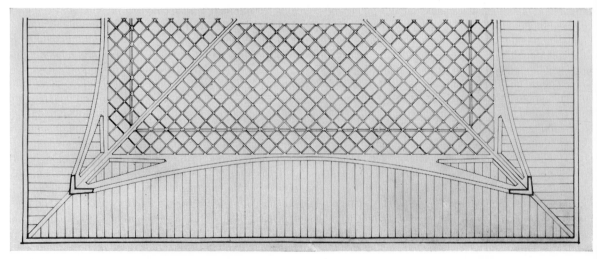

38. Exhibition Building, Salone C. Ceiling plan, from below.

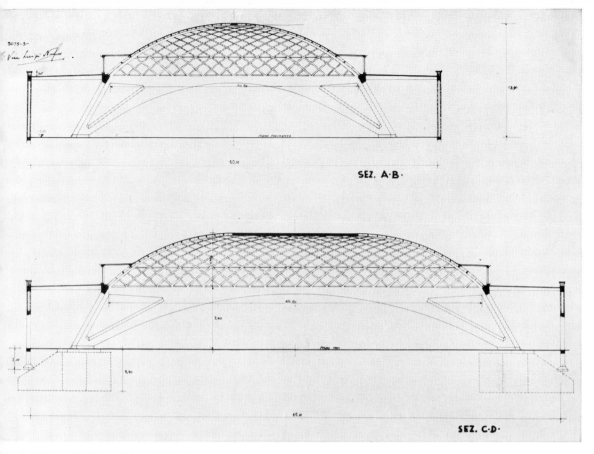

SEZ. A·B·

SEZ. C·D·

39. Exhibition Building, Salone C. Sections.

40. Exhibition Building, Salone C. Sections.

42. Exhibition Building, Salone C. One of the pre-cast supporting arches of the interior.

41. Exhibition Building, Salone C. Roof in construction.

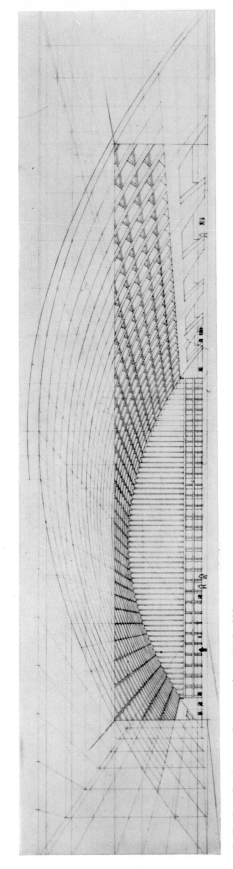

43. Project for hangar, Buenos Aires, 1949. 590' span.

44. Warehouses for salt, Tortona, 1950–51. 27 parabolic arches at 16′ 5″ intervals along a total length of 426′; 80′ span.

45. Warehouses for salt. Ceiling of prefabricated units joined by poured-in-place network (opposite page).

47. Domed ceiling for hall. Prefabricated pans in place, before pouring.

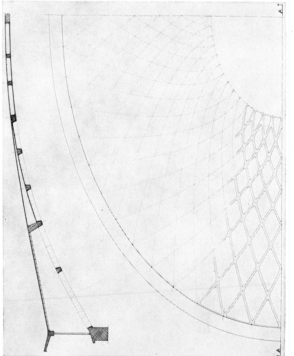

46. Domed ceiling for hall, Baths at Chianciano, 1942. Architectural design: Mario Loreti and Mario Marchi.

48. Domed ceiling for hall. Ceiling completed (opposite page).

49. Tobacco factory, Bologna, 1951–52. 700′ x 80′ x 90′.

50. Tobacco factory. Interior.

1. Tobacco factory. Interior.

52. Tobacco factory. In construction: re-usable Ferro-cemento ceiling forms
in place for pouring.

53. Tobacco factory. Scaffolding lowered, preparatory to moving it forward to position the forms for pouring the next
bay.

54. Tobacco factory. Long view: columns and walls in process of being poured (rear); completed columns and walls ready for ceiling (foreground); completed ceiling section and forms in place for pouring another ceiling section (center).

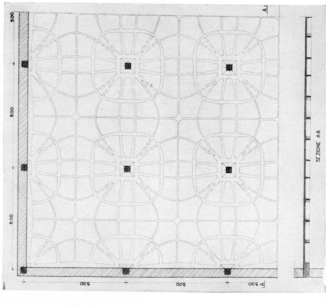

56. Gatti Wool Factory. Plan of floor slab.

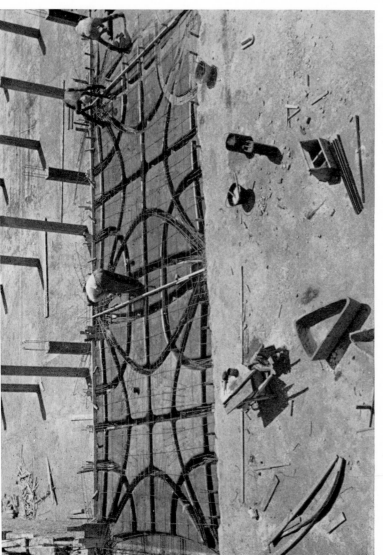

55. Gatti Wool Factory, Rome, 1951–53. Floor slab following isostatic lines of stress; utilizing re-usable, movable, Ferro-Cemento forms. View of forms in place.

57. Gatti Wool Factory. Completed ceiling (opposite page).

58. Gatti Wool Factory. Spinning mill of factory, 1953.

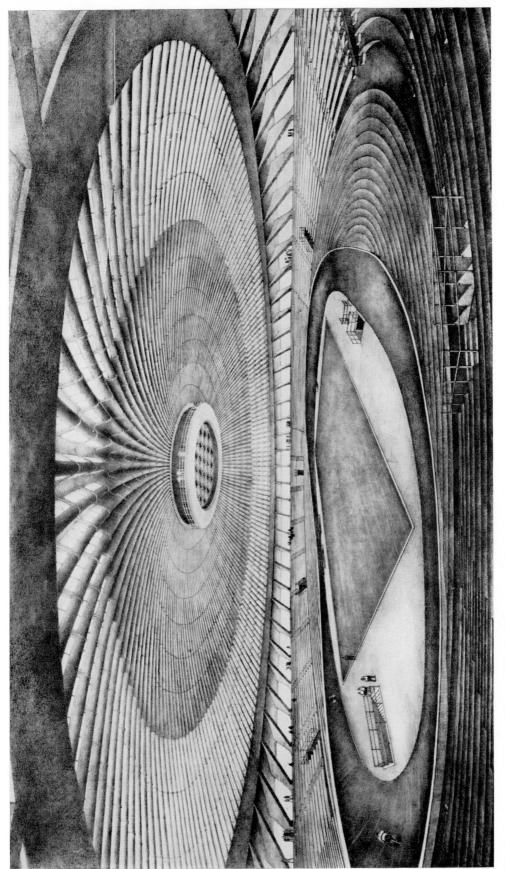

59. Project for sports palace, Vienna, 1953. Collaborating architect, Antonio Nervi.

60. Municipal Tramway, Turin, 1954. 82′ span.

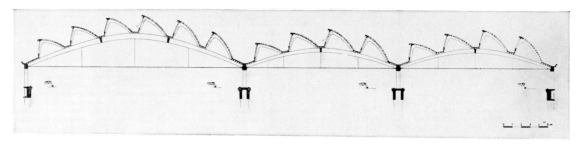

61. Municipal Tramway.

62. Municipal Tramway. Roof section.

63, 64. Storehouses, Tobacco factory, Bologna, 1954.

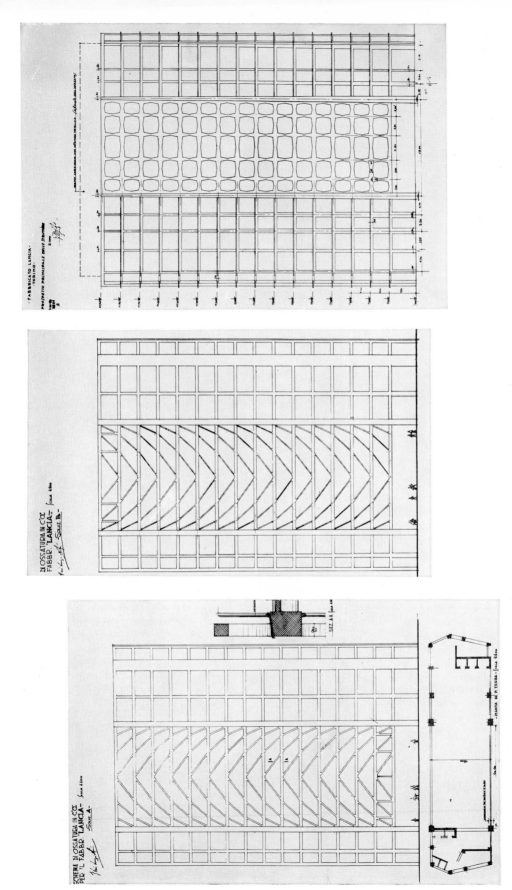

65, 66, 67. Alternate proposals for project for Lancia Factory, Turin, 1953.

68. Central Station, Naples, 1954. In collaboration with Giuseppe Vaccaro and Mario Campanella.

69. Central Station. Elevation of exterior.

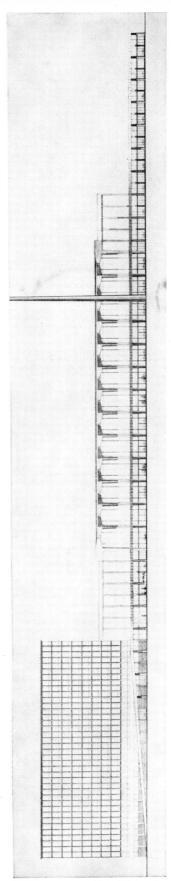

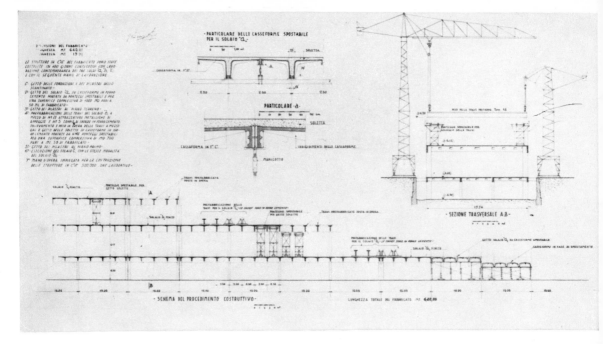

70. Factory for Fiat N.A.N., Turin, 1955. 2100' x 66'. Diagram shows procedure for raising and installing prefabricated beams (top right), and the method of constructing the factory (bottom). Movable, re-usable Ferro-cemento forms were used for pouring the first ceiling-floor slab; the prefabricated beams were hoisted in place and joined by site-poured units, also from re-usable forms, for the second and third floor ceilings. Prefabrication of beams proceeded on already completed sections of the first floor slab.

71. Factory for Fiat. Beams being raised.

72. Factory for Fiat. Beams in place.

73. Factory for Fiat. Preparing the Ferro-cemento forms for the pre-cast reinforced concrete beam.

74. Factory for Fiat. Forms ready for pouring.

75. Factory for Fiat. Completed beam.

76. Factory for Fiat A.O.P., Turin, 1954. Prefabricated trusses used instead of beams. Pre-cast truss on ground.

77. Factory for Fiat. Pre-cast trusses in place.

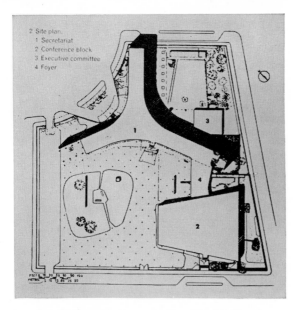

2 Site plan.
1 Secretariat
2 Conference block
3 Executive committee
4 Foyer

78. UNESCO Headquarters, Paris, 1953–57. Site plan.

79. UNESCO Headquarters. View as seen from the Eiffel Tower.

0. UNESCO Headquarters. Left, Secretariat; right, Conference Building.

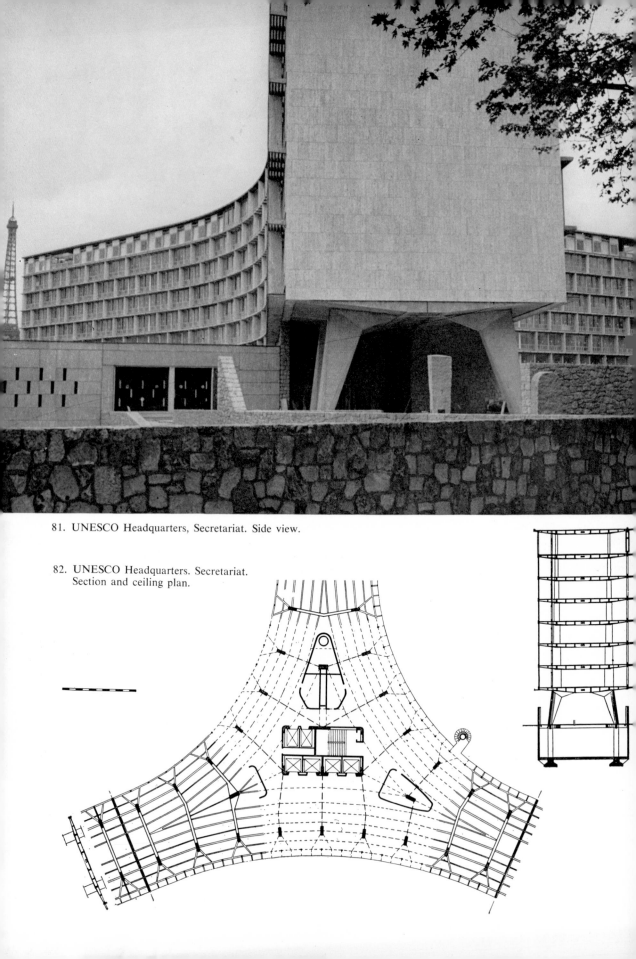

81. UNESCO Headquarters, Secretariat. Side view.

82. UNESCO Headquarters. Secretariat.
Section and ceiling plan.

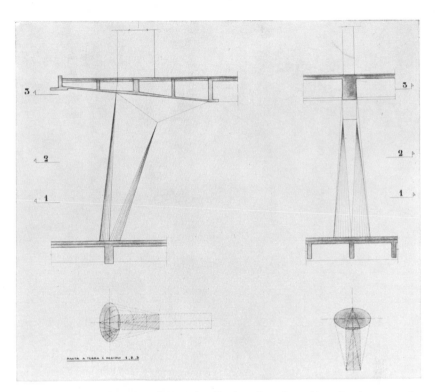

83. UNESCO Headquarters, Secretariat. Section plan of corridor, showing supports with warped surfaces.

84. UNESCO Headquarters, Secretariat. Concrete supports.

85. UNESCO Headquarters, Secretariat.
Facade at night, showing canopy.

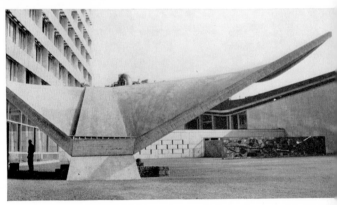

86. UNESCO Headquarters,
Secretariat. Section of canopy.

87. UNESCO Headquarters,
Secretariat. Side view of
canopy.

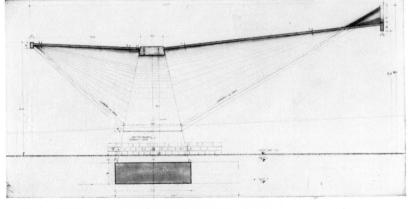

8. UNESCO Headquarters, Secretariat. Detail of facade.

9. UNESCO Headquarters, Secretariat. Exterior stairway.

90. UNESCO Headquarters, Conference Building.

91. UNESCO Headquarters, Conference Building. Sections.

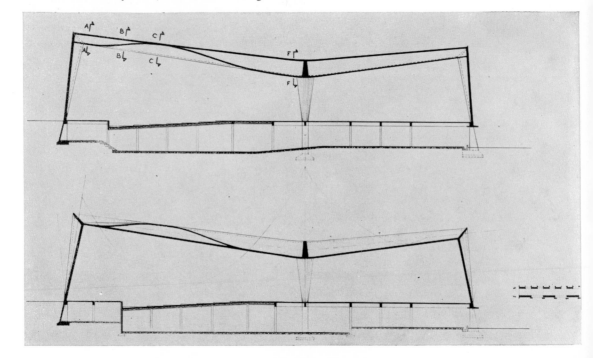

92. UNESCO Headquarters, Conference Building. Interior showing folded slab construction.

93. UNESCO Headquarters, Conference Building. Detail of roof, interior.

94. UNESCO Headquarters, Conference Building. Plan of roof.

95. UNESCO Headquarters, Conference Building. Interior.

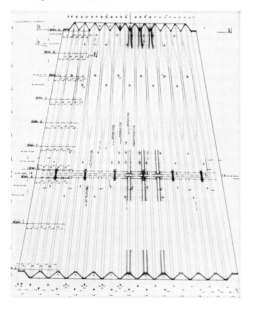

96, 97. Model of project for bridge over the river Tenza, 1955. Maximum height of roadway, 164'; to be erected with movable scaffolding.

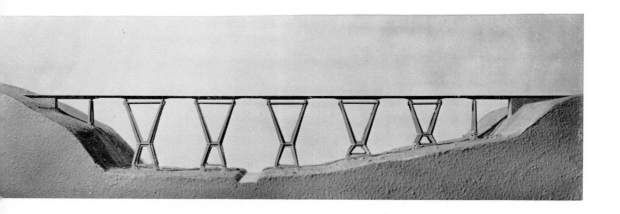

98. Pirelli Building, Milan, 1955–59. Designed in collaboration with Gio Ponti and Alberto Rosselli, architects; Antonio Fornaroli, Guiseppe Valtolina, Egidio dell'Orto, Arturo Danusso, engineers.

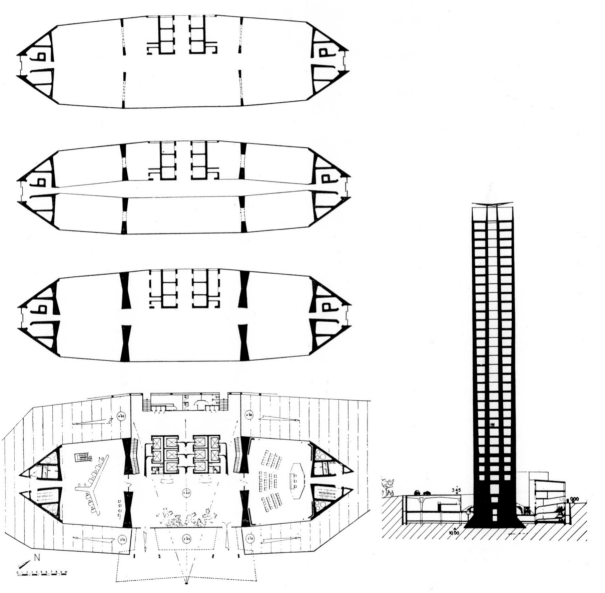

99. Pirelli Building. Plans and section. A reinforced concrete skeleton—massive at the base, slender at the top—is enclosed by a curtain wall.

100. Pirelli Building. Construction detail: ceiling.

101. Pirelli Building. Construction detail: columns and beams.

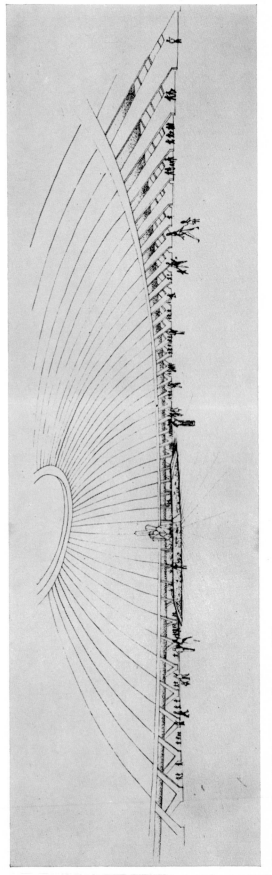

102. Project for exhibition center, Caracas, 1956.

103. 1960 Olympic buildings, Rome, Palazzetto dello Sport (small sports palace), 1958–59. Collaborating architect: Annibale Vitellozzi.

104. Palazzetto dello Sport. Exterior.

105. Palazzetto dello Sport. Plan.

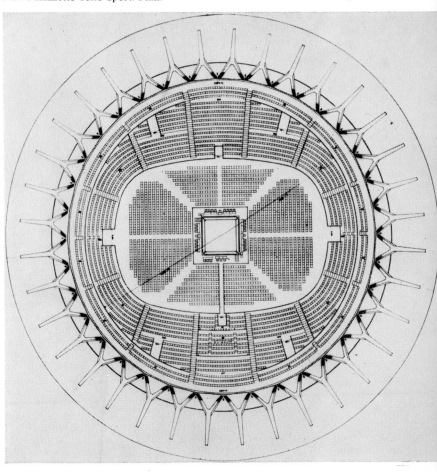

106. Palazzetto dello Sport. Prefabricated elements of the ceiling, in place for pouring.

107. Palazzetto dello Sport. Prefabricated elements on the ground.

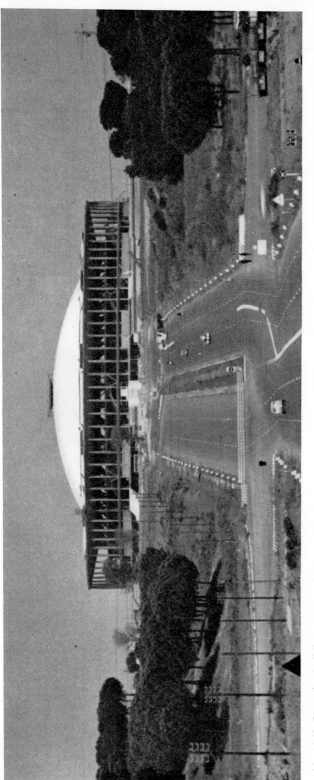

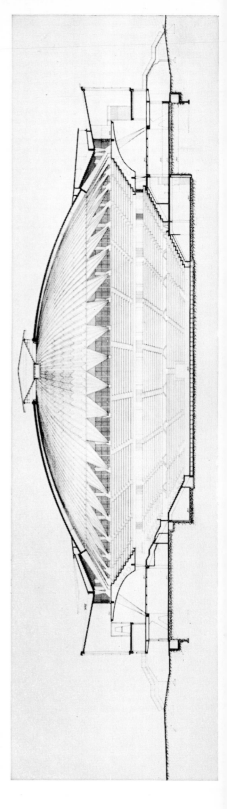

108. 1960 Olympics buildings, Rome, Palazzo dello Sport (sports palace at Universal Exposition grounds), 1959–60. Collaborating architect: Marcello Piacentini.

109. Palazzo dello Sport. Section.

110. Palazzo dello sport. Interior.

111. Palazzo dello Sport. Cupola and prefabricated roof sections.

112. Palazzo dello Sport. Fan-shaped roof elements adjoining dome of prefabricated sections.

113. Palazzo dello Sport. Section: prefabricated roof units, joined by poured-in-place reinforced concrete beams at their top and bottom points.

114. Palazzo dello Sport. Pilasters with warped surfaces, supporting dome.

115. Palazzo dello Sport. Details of pilasters.

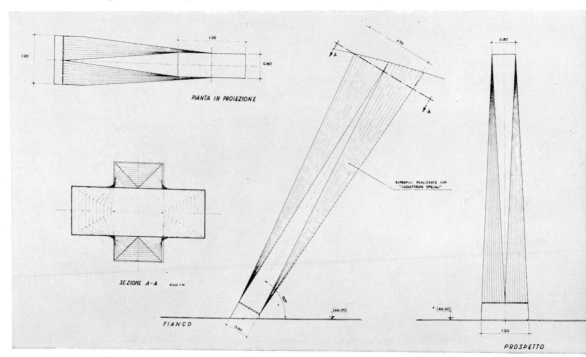

PIANTA IN PROIEZIONE

SEZIONE A-A

FIANCO

PROSPETTO

116. Palazzo dello Sport. Fan-shaped elements of dome, and tiers of seats.

117. Palazzo dello Sport. Peripheral gallery.

118, 119. 1960 Olympics buildings, Rome, Flaminio Stadium, 1957–59. Collaborating architect: Antonio Nervi. View and plan.

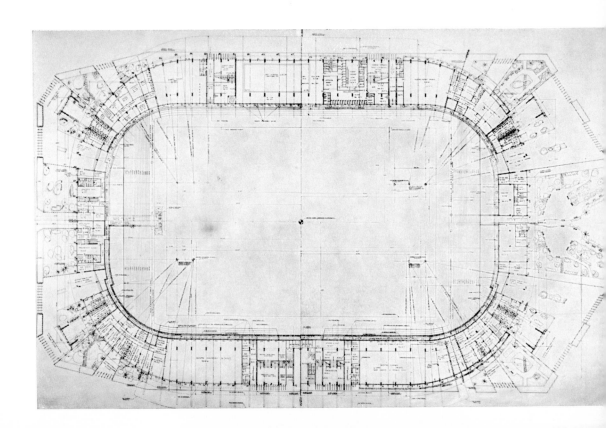

120. Flaminio Stadium. Rear detail of covered grandstand.

121. Flaminio Stadium. Grandstand in construction.

122. Flaminio Stadium. Section: grandstand frame.

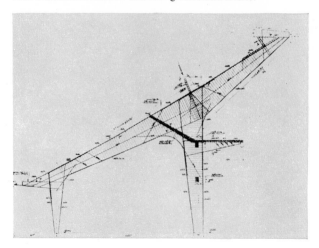

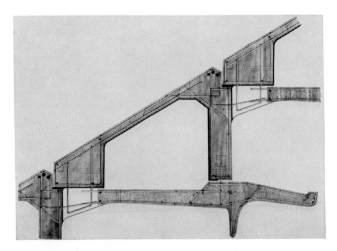

123. Flaminio Stadium. Section: prefabricated units forming seats and aisles.

124. Flaminio Stadium. Covered grandstand.

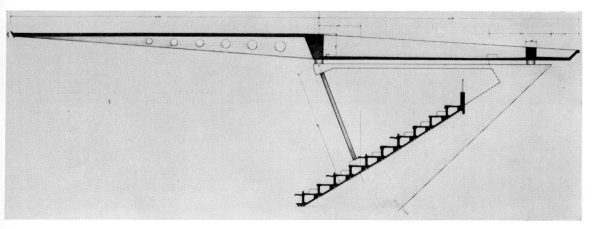

125. Flaminio Stadium. Section of the canopy which rests on each frame only at two points.

126. Flaminio Stadium. Detail of covered grandstand.

127. Project for railroad station, Savona, 1958–59. Prizewinning competition design.

128, 129. Project for Centre National des Industries et Techniques, Paris, 1955. Collaborating architects: Camelot, de Mailly, Zehrfuss; collaborating engineer for steelwork: Jean Prouvé. Three intersecting arches, each spanning 738′ and rising to a height of 158′, are joined by converging beams, for a cross-vaulted structure walled with glass. Model (above) and model of roof structure (below).

130. Project for cathedral, New Norcia, Australia, 1959. Collaborating architects: Antonio Nervi and Carlo Vannoni; collaborating engineer: Francesco Vacchini. Model of building. Triangular base, 240′ long on each side; three approximately 100′ high parabaloid vaults of 115′ span.

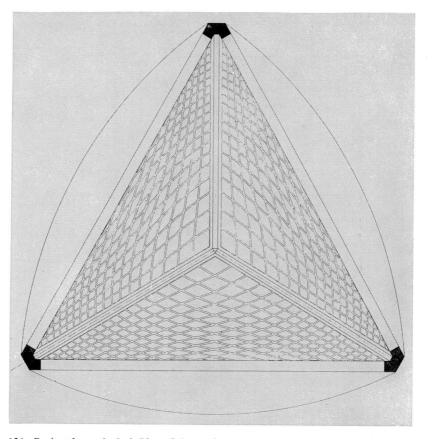

131. Project for cathedral. Plan of the roof structure seen from below.

132. Project for cathedral. Model of roof structure.

NOTES TO THE TEXT

1. Nervi's preface to *The Works of Pier Luigi Nervi,* New York, Frederick A. Praeger, 1957.
2. Alberti, Leon Battista, "On the Process of Building," from *Architectura,* (1451–52), James Leoni translation, London, 1755.
3. Viollet-le-Duc, Eugène Emmanuel, *Rational Building;* translation of article on "Construction" in the *Dictionnaire raisonné de l'architecture française,* New York and London, Macmillan and Company, 1895.
4. Nervi, Pier Luigi, *Structures,* New York, F. W. Dodge Corp., 1956. (Translation of Nervi's *Costruire correttamente,* by Giuseppina and Mario Salvadori.) p. 11.
5. Nervi, Pier Luigi, *Costruire correttamente,* Milan, Ulrico Hoepli, 1955.
6. Nervi, *Structures,* p. 26.
7. Nervi, *Scienza o arte del costruire?,* Rome, Edizioni della Bussola, 1945.
8. Nervi, *Structures,* p. 17.
9. Nervi, unpublished manuscript, 1956.
10. Ibid.
11. Nervi, *Structures,* p. 28.
12. Ibid., p. 30.
13. Alberti, op. cit.; ". . . in all Manner of Vaults, let them be of what Kind they will, we ought to imitate Nature, who, when she has knit the Bones, fastens the Flesh with Nerves, interweaving it everywhere with Ligatures, running in Breadth, Length, Height and circularly." Note, also, Nervi's words in speaking of reinforcement of concrete (*Structures,* p. 39): "The pattern of steel should always have an esthetic quality and give the impression of its being a nervous system capable of bringing life to the dead mass of concrete."
14. Nervi, unpublished manuscript cited.
15. The author, in "Reinforced-concrete construction, the work of Ernest L. Ransome, 1884–1911," *Progressive Architecture,* September, 1957, has given a summary of commercial reinforced concrete development in the United States, based on the re-discovery of Ransome's work, changing the dating of the large-scale reinforced

concrete factory in America, a phenomenon previously attributed primarily to Albert Kahn. Kahn's Packard plant, which followed Ransome's United Shoe Machinery plant, and the later Highland Park plant for Henry Ford were treated in *Progressive Architecture,* "Factory for Packard Motor Car Company—1905," October, 1957, and "Factory for Ford Motor Company—1904-14," Ibid., November, 1957.

16. Ransome patented the "Ransome System of Unit Construction" in 1909. John E. Conzelman, responsible for the "Unit System" of the Unit Construction Company, St. Louis, Mo., took out more than 51 patents between 1910 and 1916.
17. Nervi, unpublished manuscript cited.
18. Statement of Nervi to the author, August, 1959.
19. All of the following descriptions, unless otherwise noted, are from a speech given by Nervi in London, October 1955, sponsored by the I.S.E. and the Joint Committee on Structural Concrete, published in full as "Developments in Structural Technique," in *The Architect's Journal,* London, October 20, 1955. The Praeger volume already cited and G. E. Kidder Smith's book, *Italy Builds,* New York, Reinhold, 1955, contain excellent descriptive material on Nervi's work, some of which supplements the treatment here.
20. Architects Biscaretti and Ruffia collaborated on aspects of this projects, restoring the war-damaged sections and integrating them with the new structure.
21. This paragraph on Nervi's esthetic attitudes from his preface to the Praeger volume.
22. Article cited in *The Architect's Journal,* London, October 20, 1955.
23. Giedion, Sigfried, *Space, Time and Architecture,* Cambridge, The Harvard University Press, 1947; discussion of Robert Maillart's work and modern esthetics, pp. 379-84.
   Oestreich, Dieter, "Some Modern Approaches to the Problem of Form," *Industrial Design,* (translated by Edith Gilmore), July, 1959.
24. Nervi, Unpublished manuscript cited.
25. Ibid.

LIST OF WORKS

1926–27	Cinema Augusteo, Naples
1930–32	Municipal Stadium, Florence
1930, 1932	Projects for circular hangars in reinforced concrete and steel
1932	Project for 984 foot tower "Monumento della Bandiera," Monte Mario, Rome; collaborating architect: Rubens Magnani
1932–35	Project for stadium, Rome; collaborating engineer: Cesare Valle
1934	Project for a revolving house
1935–36	Project for Biedano Valley bridge, Viterbo
1935–38	Hangar for Italian Air Force, design I
1937–42	Underground storage tanks for gasoline
1938	Project for silos for the Soc. Solvay, Rosignano
1939	Project for viaduct
1940–43	Hangar for Italian Air Force, design II
1940	Project for the Pavilion of Italian Civilization for the unrealized Esposizione Universale of 1942; in collaboration with P. M. Bardi.
1940	Project for the Palace of Water and Light, for the 1942 Exposition.
1942–43	400 ton ship of reinforced concrete
1942–43	Project for a 984 foot span
1943	Project for 660 foot span for a railroad station
1945	Project for bridge over the Arno, Florence
1945	Warehouse of Ferro-cemento, Rome.
1945	Project for factory
1946	Project for Palermo Central Station
1946	Project for prefabricated circular house
1947	Conte Trossi wharf, San Michele di Pagano, Genoa; collaborating architect: Luigi Carlo Daneri
1947–49	Swimming pool for Naval Academy, Leghorn
1948–50	Project for air-insulated shed roof
1948–49	Exhibition Building, Turin, "Salone B"

1949–50	Exhibition Building, Turin, "Salone C"
1949	Project for hangar, Buenos Aires
1950	Restaurant roof, Kursaal beach casino, Ostia; collaborating architect: Attilio La Padula
1950–51	Warehouses for salt, Tortona
1951	Project for bridge over the Reno river, Sasso Marconi; collaborating engineer: Carlo Castelli-Guidi
1951–52	Tobacco factory, Bologna
1951–53	Gatti wool factory, Rome
1952–53	Pressure pipeline, "System Nervi"
1952	Ceiling, Baths at Chianciano; collaborating architects: Mario Loreti and Mario Marchi
1953	Project for Sports Palace, Vienna; in collaboration with Antonio Nervi
1953	Project for Lancia factory, Turin
1954	Municipal Tramway, Turin
1954	Storehouses, Tobacco factory, Bologna
1954	Central Station, Naples; in collaboration with Giuseppe Vaccaro and Mario Campanella
1953–57	UNESCO headquarters, Paris; collaborating architects: Marcel Breuer and Bernard Zehrfuss
1954–55	Fiat factories, Turin
1955	Project for bridge over the river Tenza
1955	Project for "Centre National des Industries et Techniques," Paris
1955–59	Pirelli Building, Milan; in collaboration with Gio Ponti and Alberto Rosselli, architects; Antonio Fornaroli, Giuseppe Valtolina, Egidio dell'Orto, Arturo Danusso, engineers.
1956	Project for exhibition center, Caracas
1956–57	1960 Olympics buildings, Rome; small Sports palace; collaborating architect: Antonio Vitellozzi
1958–59	1960 Olympics buildings, large Sports Palace; collaborating architect: Marcello Piacentini
1957–59	1960 Olympics Buildings, Flaminio Stadium; in collaboration with Antonio Nervi
1958–59	Project for railroad station, Savona
1959	Project for cathedral, New Norcia, Australia
1959	Project for elevated roadway, Rome

BRIEF CHRONOLOGY

1891	Born June 21, Sondrio, Italy
1913	Graduated from Civil Engineering School, Bologna
1913–15	Worked in the Technical Office of the Società per Costruzioni Cementizie, Bologna
1915–18	Officer, Engineering Corps, World War I
1918–23	Worked with Società per Costruzioni Cementizie, Florence
1920–32	Own firm, Soc. Ing. Nervi e Nebbiosi, Rome
1932–present	Soc. Igg. Nervi e Bartoli, Rome

HONORS

1947–present	Professor of Technology and Structural Techniques, School of Architecture, University of Rome
1950	Honorary Doctor of Architecture, University of Buenos Aires
1955	Certificate of Commendation, Institution of Structural Engineers, London
1956	Honorary member of the American Institute of Architects
1957	Honorary member of the Academy of Arts and Letters, National Institute of Arts and Letters, New York
1957	Honorary member of the Royal Beaux Arts Academy, Stockholm
1957	Brown Medal of the Franklin Institute, Philadelphia
1957	Exener Medal of the Oesterreiche Gewerbevereines, Vienna
1958	Gold Medal of the Philadelphia Chapter of the American Institute of Architects
1958	Gold Medal of the Confederazione Generale Italiana Professionisti—Artisti, Rome

BIBLIOGRAPHY OF BOOKS AND ARTICLES WRITTEN BY PIER LUIGI NERVI (in Chronological Order, 1931–1959)

BOOKS

Arte o scienza del costruire, Edizione della Bussola, Rome, 1945.

El lenguaye Arquitectonico (Lectures given at the School of Architecture, University of Buenos Aires, published by the Ministry of Education).

Costruire correttamente, Edizioni Hoepli, Milan, 1954.

Structures, F. W. Dodge, New York, 1956.

ARTICLES

"Arte e tecnica del costruire," *Quadrante,* No. 2 (Soc. Grafica G. Modiano), Milan, June, 1931.

"Pensieri sull'ingegneria," *Quadrante,* No. 6, October, 1932.

"Monumento alla bandiera," *Quadrante,* No. 8, December, 1933.

"Una casa girevole," *Quadrante,* No. 13.

"Problemi della realizzazione architettonica," *Casabella,* No. 74, Milan, February, 1934.

"Una aviorimessa in cemento armato," *Casabella,* No. 124, April, 1938.

"Considerazioni sulle lezioni della cupola di S. Maria del Fiore e sulle probabili cause di esse," *Rilievi e studi sulla cupola del Brunelleschi,* Tipografia Ettore Rinaldi, Florence, 1939.

"La tecnica e i nuovi orientamenti estetici," (Atti convegno di ingegneria dell'anno XVIII), VII Triennale, Milan.

"Un arco monumentale in conglomerato non armato," *Casabella,* No. 176, August, 1942.

"Le basi della ricostruzione," *Ricerca Scientifica e Ricostruzione,* July, 1945.

"Corretto costruire," *Strutture,* No. 1, Ed. della Bussola, April, 1947.

"Economia edilizia," *La Casa,* Instituto Grafico Tiberino, Rome, April, 1950.

"La estructuras resistentes del palacio Exposition de Turin," *La Ingenieria,* No. 8, 1949.

"Nouvelle Hall du palais des Exposition à Turin," *Architecture d'aujourd'hui,* No. 27, December, 1949.

"Ancora sul senso dell'architettura," *Domus,* March 1950.

"Le costruzioni navali in ferro-cemento," *Industria Italiana del Cemento,* No. 7–8, 1950.

"Il ferro-cemento sue caratteristiche e possibilità," *L'Ingegnere,* No. 1, 1951 (Ed. Istituto della Propaganda Internazionale), Milan.

"The reinforced concrete members from Turin exhibition hall," *Civil Engineering* 1, 1951.

"La resistenza per forma—caratteristica statico—architettonica del cemento armato," *Rivista Pirelli,* August, 1951.

"Le proporzioni nella tecnica," *Domus,* No. 264–65, December, 1951.

"Possibilità costruttive ed architettoniche della pre-fabbricazione strutturale," *Architettura,* Cantiere No. 1, 1952.

"Precast concrete offers new possibilities for design of shell structures," *Journal of the America Concrete Institute,* No. 6, February, 1953.

"L'Architecture du beton armé et le problème des coffrages," *L'Architecture d'Aujourd'hui,* No. 48, July, 1953.

"Precast concrete offers new possibilities in design of shell structures," *Civil Engineering,* February, 1953.

"Considerations for a curriculum," *Student Publication of the School of Design North Carolina State College,* Raleigh, Vol. 4, No. 2, 1954.

"Costruire correttamente," *Casabella,* No. 202, 1954.

"Concrete and structural form," (Lecture at the Friends Meeting House, Euston Road, London), on Friday, 14th October, 1955.

"Concrete and structural form," *The Structural Engineer,* No. 5, May, 1956.

"The place of structure in architecture," *Architectural Record,* July, 1956.

"Kleine Sporthalle für die Olympischen Spiele in Rom 1960," *Bauwelt,* No. 49, December, 1957.

"Critica delle strutture," *Casabella,* No. 223, January, 1959.

"Critica delle strutture" (Cinque ponti), *Casabella,* No. 224, February, 1959.

"Critica delle strutture" (Rapporti tra Ingegneria e Architettura), *Casabella,* No. 225, March, 1959.

"Le strutture dell'Unesco," *Casabella,* No. 226, April, 1959.

"Critica delle strutture," (Modello e imitazione), *Casabella,* No. 227, May, 1959.

SELECTED BIBLIOGRAPHY ON PIER LUIGI NERVI
(in Chronological Order, 1932-1959)

Giovanni Michelucci, "Lo stadio Giovanni Berta in Firenze," *Architettura,* 1932.

Gaston Abraham, "Le Stade G. Berta à Florence," *La Technique des Travaux,* February, 1933.

P. M. Bardi, "Lo Stadio di Firenze," *Casabella,* April, 1933.

"Concorso per l'auditorium di Roma," *Architettura,* December, 1935.

"Nuovi tipi di Aviorimesse," *Architettura,* March, 1938.

"Le halle du palais des Expositions Turin," *La Technique des Travaux,* No. 9-10, 1949.

E. Pellegrini, "Strutture Palazzo Torino Esposizione," *Domus,* No. 231, 1948.

Alfredo Villalonga, "Pier Luigi Nervi," *Rivista de Arquitectura,* October, 1950.

Libero de Libero, "Saper costruire," *Rivista "Pirelli,"* August, 1951.

"Le palais des Expositions de Turin," *Batir,* October, 1951.

Mario Palmieri, "Boldness typifies Italian precast design," *Concrete,* May, 1952.

A. L. Huxtable, "Geodetic and plastic expressions abroad," *Progressive Architecture,* June, 1953.

"Pier Luigi Nervi," *Architectural Forum,* November, 1953.

Giovanni M. Cosco, "Espacialidad y estructura en las arquitectura moderna y obra de Pier Luigi Nervi," *Arquitectura Mexico,* December, 1953.

Hilda Selem, "Pier Luigi Nervi och Haus Verk," *Byggmastaren—Byggnadsteknik,* B 12, 1953.

Yuichi Ino (Editor), *World's Contemporary Architecture,* No. 9, Tokyo, 1953.

G. Perugini, "Pier Luigi Nervi," *Rassegna Critica di Architettura,* No. 30, 1954.

"Sport palast di Vienna," *Sele Arte,* No. 13, August, 1954.

Luigi Vagnetti, "Pier Luigi Nervi o la estruttura hecha forma," *Informes de la Construccion,* November, 1954.

C. G. Argan, *Pier Luigi Nervi,* Ediz. II Balcone, Milan, 1955.

"Nervi," *Concrete Quarterly,* No. 25, April–June, 1955.

"Concrete and structural form," *The Architects Journal,* October, 1955.

"Concrete and structural form," *Engineering,* October, 1955.

"Concrete and structural form," *Concrete and Constructional Engineering,* November, 1955.

"Concrete and structural form," *The Architect and Building News,* October, 1955.

G. E. Kidder-Smith, *Italy Builds,* Reinhold, New York, 1955.

"Pier Luigi Nervi—Ingenieur und Architekt," *Werk,* October, 1956.

"Pier Luigi Nervi," Ein Gestalterdes Stahlbetons, *Baukunst und Werkform,* No. 10, 1956.

Fredrik Fogh, "Pier Luigi Nervi," *Arkitekten,* No. 14, 1957.

"Bigningsstatikkens forhold til arkitekturen au P. L. Nervi," *Bygg Tidsskrift for Husbygging,* No. 2, February, 1957.

Andrzej Brandt, "Pier Luigi Nervi—Architekt i konstruktor," *Inzynieria i Budownicctwo,* No. 10, 1957.

"Italy; the story of a visit to northern Italy in October 1956," *Concrete Quarterly,* No. 32, 1957.

Pier Luigi Nervi, Verlag Gerd Hatje, Stuttgart, 1957. (American edition, *The Works of Pier Luigi Nervi,* Frederick A. Praeger, New York, 1957.)

"Una struttura di Pier Luigi Nervi," *Zodiac,* October, 1957.

"Poetry in concrete," *Time,* November, 1957.

Achille Perilli, "Pier Luigi Nervi," *Civiltà delle Macchine,* January, February, 1958.

"Pier Luigi Nervi—Palacio de los deportes en Roma," *Informes de la Costruccion,* February, 1958.

"Il Palazzetto dello Sport a Roma," *L'Architettura,* January, 1958.

"La siege de l'UNESCO à Paris," *L'Architecture d'aujourd'hui,* December, 1958.

"UNESCO's cheerful new home," *Architectural Forum,* December, 1958.

"Le nouveau Palais de l'UNESCO à Paris," *La Technique des Travaux,* January, 1959.

"Der Palazetto in Rom—P. L. Nervi," *Deutsche Architektur,* March, 1959.

Allan Temko, "The world's most daring builder," *Horizon,* No. 3, 1959.

"The human world of Nervi," *Architectural Record,* April, 1959.

SOURCES OF ILLUSTRATIONS

Barsotti, Florence: 6
Gilles Ehrmann, Seine, France: 90, 95
Fototecnica Publifoto, Gautiere Pirelli: 100, 101
G. Gherardi; A. Fiorelli, Rome: 104, 105, 108, 112, 118, 121, 125, 132
Lucien Hervé, Paris: 84
Laboratorio Fotografico, Rome: 70, 71, 72, 73, 74, 75, 76, 77, 92, 106, 107
Moisio, Turin: 36, 60, 62
Riccardo Moncalvo, Turin: 26, 28, 30, 32, 33, 34, 35, 40, 41, 44, 45
Courtesy UNESCO, New York: Beretty, 81; Lajoux, 80; Laloux, 85, 93; Ribaud, 79; Volta, 86
Vasari, Rome: 7, 8, 9, 10, 11, 12, 14, 15, 16, 18, 22, 23, 24, 25, 29, 31, 38, 39, 46, 48. 55, 56, 59, 65, 66, 67, 123, 128, 129
Vera Fotografia: 98

INDEX

The numerals in *italics* refer to the illustrations.